'At last, a book on solution focused team coaching. simple and elegant.' – Peter Szabó, member of the ICF coach assessment team, co-author with Insoo Kim Berg of *Brief Coaching for Lasting Solutions*.

'The SolutionCircle *is a simple, powerful and practical way of working with teams. In just one coaching session, a Board of Directors achieved a huge amount of visible progress towards an important business goal. And this process took less than half a day!'* – Rob Rave, The Solutions Game.

'Insightful in approach, resourceful in ideas, practical in application, this excellent book meets the needs of both the experienced coach and the manager looking fornew and innovative ways of developing teams ...' – Shaun Lincoln, Director of Coaching and Mentoring, Centre for Excellence in Leadership.

'One of the most practical books on team coaching – a goldmine of information and application. It clearly explains Solutions Focus and the SolutionCircle, with relevant and illuminating case studies, numerous instantly applicable tools and comprehensive session plans. I will start incorporating the ideas and techniques into my work immediately.'* Janine Waldman, The Solutions Focus.

'Daniel has done a formidable job; a service for anyone who is seriously interested in working with teams in a solution-focused manner. The book gives you the steps of the dance. Follow these steps and you will be amazed how this simple – yet profound – approach can help you help teams achieve their goals in ways that are not only effective but fun at the same time.'* – Ben Furman. Author of *Solution Talk* and inventor of the Reteaming method.

Team Coaching with the SolutionCircle

Team Coaching with the SolutionCircle

A practical guide to solutions focused team development

Daniel Meier

Solutions Focus at Work Series

solutions books

First published in Great Britain in 2005 by
SolutionsBooks
26 Christchurch Road
Cheltenham
Gl50 2PL
United Kingdom

Originally published in Germany in 2004 by SolutionSurfers
as Wege zur Erfolgreichen Teamentwicklung mit dem
SolutionCircle
(ISBN 3-8334-0668-2)

UK ISBN 0 954 9749 1 3

Translated by Kirsten Dierolf and Jenny Clarke

Cover design by
Cathi Stevenson

Graphics by
Daniela Kienzler

Design, typesetting and production by
Action Publishing Technology Ltd

Printed in Great Britain

The New Wave of Change is in SolutionsBooks!

In the 1960s, the legendary record label Impulse! launched itself with the motto 'The New Wave of Jazz is on Impulse!'. The label became the home of legends like John Coltrane and Charles Mingus, and led the way for a whole movement of new musical forms and talent.

In the same way, we now announce that the new wave of change is in SolutionsBooks! We will be promoting the developing movement around Solutions Focus and other positive, minimal change technologies including narrative and Appreciative Inquiry, which value simplicity and pragmatism over complex models and ill-founded theory.

This new wave is not simply another model for change – it is a different *kind* of approach. We are not interested in finding grand designs. Instead, we seek ways to find the direct routes to progress, to explore the fine line between what matters and what can be overlooked, in helping people and organisations move forwards in a complex and fluid world.

Solutions Focus is built on the successful field of Solution Focused Brief Therapy (SFBT) as developed by Steve de Shazer and Insoo Kim Berg at the Brief Family Therapy Center, Milwaukee. Over the past fifteen years SFBT practitioners have discovered the power of finding what works, staying at the surface, careful listening and building on small successes, and bypassing conventional therapeutic tools such as diagnosis, cause analysis, 'talking through' the problem and searching for repressed feelings and thoughts.

This radically simple, skilful and subtle practice is found in randomised controlled studies to give as good or better results than more conventional methods, but in less time and with greater satisfaction from clients. Practitioners report fewer features of burn-out than with other approaches. We seek to continue this movement into the worlds of organisations, businesses and other settings.

Some people have found the ideas presented here to be simplistic – nice and positive, just like PollyAnna. We think this misses the point: simple is *not* simplistic. To be less simple, to take less direct routes involving a priori problem analysis, weakness diagnosis and any of the other myriad potential excursions and pitfalls, is to risk at best expending more resources and time than necessary, and at worst spreading confusion and making any problems significantly worse.

Ludwig Wittgenstein wrote that the aim of philosophy was 'to show the fly the way out of the fly-bottle'. In promoting the new wave of change, our aim is show how simplicity and clarity can minimise confusion and futile effort. Readers will be better equipped to find their own ways out of bottles.

Mark McKergow and Jenny Clarke
SolutionsBooks
www.solutionbooks.com

Contents

Preface

'The solution does not care where the problem came from.'

W. Herren

This paradoxical quote is a powerful maxim for dealing productively with conflicts in teams. When co-workers fight, when team members are not co-operating, or when change processes get stuck, what usually happens is that the situation is analysed thoroughly and the causes and culprits are identified. A lot of meetings are characterised by extensive analysis of the problem.

The SolutionCircle turns this procedure and the underlying way of thinking upside down and shows how teams can be more efficient and more productive.

This book is an invitation

You are invited to learn about a simple yet effective way of developing a team sustainably and systematically – even in turbulent situations. In many ways the SolutionCircle presents a paradigm shift when it comes to working with groups:

Instead of asking 'why' in difficult situations, in the SolutionCircle we are interested in 'where'!

Instead of investing a lot of time and energy in a thorough analysis of the problem, in the SolutionCircle we consistently concentrate on our experiences of past success and use that as a basis for building solutions.

Instead of trying to eliminate deficits in the team, in the SolutionCircle we aim at taking new steps based on existing strengths, competencies and skills.

The SolutionCircle came out of my coaching experience. In my work as a coach for various companies, I often had insufficient time to work with teams in difficult situations. So, I started looking for ideas and methods which would enable me to improve complex team situations, sustainably and with an appreciative mindset.

I was guided by the following ideas in the search for useful approaches:

- I am less interested in theoretical models than in concrete ideas that have been tried and tested in real life. I was interested in what works in the day-to-day life of teams.
- Utilising tools that centre the energies of the team on the solution is important to me. I have often been in situations where individuals or whole groups of people are stuck in suffering and complaining. Team meetings and breaks are used to list the shortcomings and the mismanagement – but the crucial step toward a solution is not taken. I have worked with teams confronted with change situations of vital importance who, nevertheless, remained immobilised – in resignation, wanting to keep everything just the way it was.
- I look for ways of achieving more in a team than merely overcoming a difficult situation or solving a problem. In turbulent situations, the team can also find a great opportunity for further development of the team. It is the aim of this method to take this opportunity and use it productively!
- What I was looking for was a simple and reasonable method, which could be accessible to people without much background knowledge. I searched for tools which could be used

effectively in various situations by every team leader, every manager and even by the team members themselves.

- What I also wanted desperately was that my work with teams should produce results which could then be implemented. In my mind's eye, I saw dozens of cards with team rules and team analyses, with measures derived from these analyses parading in front of me. I have been in many workshops on team development, performance improvement, and crisis intervention as team member and as team leader – but when I think of all the flipcharts with all the measures and then compare that with what was actually implemented, the yield is not very impressive. This is why I wanted to find out how teams can succeed in moving in a desired direction toward their goals together.

The Brief Therapy Model

My model is founded on the solution- and resource-oriented working model developed by Steve de Shazer and Insoo Kim Berg at the Brief Therapy Center in Milwaukee (USA). As family therapists, they were looking for ways of helping couples in a shorter period with the same or better results. By concentrating on solutions, they were able to lower the average time of the consultancy by over 70% reaching the same success rate as traditional forms of therapy. The centre of their conversations with their clients was not an elaborate theoretical model but a thorough analysis of methods that had already proven successful in their daily work. Various interventions and conversations were observed carefully and evaluated using this perspective: which questions and interventions produce useful results in the lives of the clients? The solution-oriented working model was developed from research on the efficacy of consultation. More recently, this way of conducting a conversation has been developed further not only in therapy but also for coaching individuals in companies and as the basis for the method of working with teams described here.

The SolutionCircle

The method put forward in this book is called 'SolutionCircle'. This label and the approach behind it rests on the development of a clear and realistic picture of the desired future for the team: a common image of future team work that promises to be interesting, effective, fun and goal-oriented. We consistently align ourselves with the desired goals – and not with the problems that could prevent us from getting there! In order to achieve this, it is vital that we work with, focus on and shed light on the existing resources – they are the ground in which the desired future can grow.

I wanted to create a little book that provides you, dear reader, with a good overview of the method, that you can read relatively quickly, and that can help you decide whether you want to learn more about the SolutionCircle. I hope that I have achieved this goal. I hope that you and other people are inspired to integrate single elements of the SolutionCircle into your daily life; I also hope that you will experience some miraculous moments in your first careful steps using the SolutionCircle and then become ever more curious and delve deeper into the method with enthusiasm.

Hints and Tips

You will find a toolkit in the following chapters: I will introduce the four basic principles, explain each element and describe the most important tools. Many practical examples illustrate how the method works. The toolbox provides many useful hints and tips. However, hints and tips are no panacea, if only because human beings are not machines. One tip can fit one team wonderfully – and fail miserably in another situation. The reactions of human beings cannot be determined in advance and people react differently in different situations. So if you only use the hints and tips introduced in this book, you might not get very far – simply because the idea does not work in your specific situation. Whatever you do, it should fit you – it should be an expression of your attitude and convictions. Otherwise, you could be exposed as someone who does not mean what he or she says. Whatever you decide to do after reading this book – you should make it into something that suits you.

Have fun with this tool book. Use it in order to bring solution-oriented methods to teams looking for progress. Experiment with the solution-oriented questions, use the individual elements of the SolutionCircle creatively in your team meetings. Start with small steps. Let yourself be surprised by what happens. In the end, it is your own experience that counts. This book is an invitation – I hope that you accept it and you will experience the same thing that I did: you will become more courageous in using it, more dynamic and more curious. You will discover more room to act and you will achieve goals more successfully with your team.

Daniel Meier
Bremgarten, January 2004

Foreword

by Ben Furman

Daniel Meier has done a good deed for all of us by writing this highly instructive, down to earth, hands-on book on how to coach teams in a solution-focused manner.

The term 'solution-focused' is really a misnomer. In the 1970s an interesting form of brief psychotherapy emerged in the United States. This approach was based on the idea that when people consult us with problems, we should be more interested in what it is that maintains those problems than in their possible causes or origins. It was proposed that by focusing on how people try to solve their problems we can identify the mechanisms that maintain those problems and then be able to suggest alternative ways of dealing with them. It was the job of the (problem-focused) consultant to analyse problems in order to understand how they were maintained, and then to suggest another course of action that would help solve the problem – or at least to block the mechanism that was responsible for maintaining it.

However in the 1980s a novel approach to this brief therapy arrived – not based on analysing the mechanisms of problem maintenance but on analysing mechanisms of progress instead. In this approach one would not pay too much attention to what may have been perpetuating the problem – let alone to what might have been the cause of the problem. Instead we were interested in what had worked so far, even if only temporarily, to solve the problem. This approach was radically different from the problem-focused approach and deserved to have a new name. But what should you name an approach to problem solving which is not at all focused on problems but rather on what progress there exists already? Eureka! 'Solution-focused' of course! The term was a play on words. You might say that the opposite of problem-focused is solution-focused but that is not really true. A more appropriate term would have been 'progress focused' but that is even less attractive.

Yet progress focused is what this approach is all about. You engage people in a conversation about what progress they would like to see happen in their lives, you help them identify signs of progress that are already there and you help them plan the steps that they need to take to see more of the kind of progress they desire. The approach is simple, effective and time saving. Its only problem is that it is a bit too simple to be taken seriously by people who live under the assumption that simple ideas cannot be profound ideas.

Very soon it became evident that solution-focused psychology was not only good for therapy. It was a marvellous idea that could be used wherever there was a need to improve human functioning or to solve human problems, as you would say in the old way of thinking. The approach has since been picked up by a growing number of consultants, coaches, managers, teachers … you name it.

In recent years a number of creative people have successfully applied solution-focused psychology to team building and organisational development. Many of them have found a way of repackaging these ideas so that they are easier to adopt in organisational contexts. This is exactly where Daniel has succeeded. He has taken the main ingredients of the solution-focused approach and divided them into clear steps so that the approach becomes usable by anyone interested in trying it with practically any group of people.

In doing this Daniel has done a formidable job; a service for anyone who is seriously interested in working with teams in a solution-focused manner. The book gives you the steps of the dance. Follow these steps and you will be amazed how this simple – yet profound – approach can help you help teams achieve their goals in ways that are not only effective but fun at the same time.

Ben Furman

Helsinki Brief Therapy Institute, inventor of the Reteaming method

www.reteaming.com

1 Introducing the SolutionCircle

'Shoot for the moon. Even if you miss it, you will land among the stars.'

Les Brown

You are leading a team and you are looking for effective methods to reach your ambitious goals.

You notice conflicts and tension in the team and would like to deal with them or you want to recover a sense of dynamic fun and enthusiasm. This is why you are looking for an approach that will help you deal with these situations effectively and sustainably.

Your team is faced with a process of change (or is already in the process). You are looking for tools to shape this development successfully.

You are taking over a new project. Pressure for success is high – time is scarce. You are looking for a set of working principles that will enable you and your project group to work consistently in a result oriented fashion right from the start.

You want to give your team members more responsibility and would like them to develop their entrepreneurial spirit.

The SolutionCircle is a tried and tested, effective method for these and similar situations. It enables you to focus your energy and your time to developing solutions in the everyday life of the team. Instead of finding out whom to blame, complaining, or producing deficit oriented analyses, you can use the tools introduced here to conduct special workshops for working on turbulent situations in the team. Moreover, individual elements are so flexible that they can also be used in the daily life of a team in order to improve the efficiency of the meetings, for example.

The SolutionCircle for Dealing With Turbulent Situations in a Team

With the SolutionCircle, you can support teams in finding a way out of complex and tense situations. The method consists of eight elements that help you design one or several workshops to attain realistic goals. Versatile tools make it possible to apply the SolutionCircle successfully to resolve conflict and deal with unnecessary tension in the team.

The SolutionCircle in the Day-to-Day Life of a Team

As team leader or project manager, you will be repeatedly confronted with problems, big or small. Managers can use the elements described here in various team settings. The tools help you to proceed in a solution-oriented fashion – for example in defining the goal of a project, in dealing with questions in the department meeting, in conversations regarding qualifications, or in clarifying an account.

In addition, team members can find themselves in situations ranging from unstable to stormy, whether they are participating, only listening or by-standers in the conflict. Team members can also function as a kind of 'agent for solutions' and become part of the solution instead of the problem. The tools described here show how you can contribute a lot to finding a solution by asking simple questions. Sometimes a single question focused on the solution, asked at the right time, can work wonders.

The Central Idea of the SolutionCircle

The usual methods with which we work in teams assume that it is essential to analyse the problem thoroughly, so that everything concerning tension in the team is brought into the open. At the beginning of a workshop held to deal with tension and to improve collaboration, you often hear participants say that they would like to 'speak openly about the issues' – in these or similar words. What they would like to do is to analyse mistakes and weaknesses. The idea that a cleansing thunderstorm is necessary before we can work constructively at solving the problem seems to be deeply rooted in us.

One of the theoretical foundations of Change Management is that the dichotomy between what is and what is aimed for must be clearly defined. It is important to show this discrepancy so that everybody understands where the most difficult problems lie. Once detected they are analysed with utmost care: where do they come from? Who caused them? What deficits are they derived from? The results of this analysis are then presented to all employees of a company. In this way, change mangers hope to convince everybody to the last employee that there are really big problems. They want to shake up or rattle the employees so that they are then willing to change.

These approaches must be justified since they are used successfully in many places. However, the SolutionCircle proposes a different way of doing things. The central thought of the SolutionCircle is:

Change happens more sustainably, more dynamically, and more effectively when it rests on strengths.

The SolutionCircle is based on the insight that exploring potential together, shedding light on extraordinary successes and working constructively on common goals lead to faster, more democratic and more sustainable change than a deficit-oriented analysis of the faulty and problematic state of affairs. This is why understanding exactly what the problem is or analysing the deficits plays a less important role in our work. The SolutionsCircle vision is one of lively, positive, solution- and resource-oriented change.

We generally see things in one of two ways. On the one hand, we see ourselves and other people as flawed creatures with defects and deficits – thus basically imperfect and prone to mistakes. Then we focus our attention mainly on what is not working in the team and what mistakes are being made. You might recognise this situation: there are teams that have made it their team culture to criticise every flaw very openly – sometimes this goes so far that they cannot regard anything, wherever it comes from, as positive. People grouse, grin smugly and complain. In the coffee breaks, in the hallway, before and after meetings, you hear the latest hair-raising stories and complaints about constant time pressure, scarce resources, impossible working conditions and difficult colleagues. In this vale of tears, fun, innovation, the joy of experimenting and the will to perform all disappear.

On the other hand, we can discover great abilities and resources in ourselves, in other people, and in teams – potential that is so encompassing that we can hardly measure it.

We generally tend toward the first way of seeing things. We often see the flaws and not the incredible possibilities. In addition, we are inclined to blow the negative experiences out of proportion so that we then can no longer recognise all the positive experiences that make up our capability to perform. This is how we end up limiting our opportunities! Instead of shaping our future actively, we use our time to deplore the past.

The SolutionCircle builds on the basic assumption that every human being, every team and every organisation has a far bigger potential than they are usually conscious of. This potential has already flashed up occasionally in the past – at least in a few moments, sometimes over a longer period. The SolutionCircle works with this power of the potential and competencies. When we are looking back into the past in the SolutionCircle, we are not looking for mistakes and deficits, but we are exploring the competencies of the team and are searching for moments of success. This power is the basis on which we can then build solutions for the issues at hand.

When in conflict situations, people have an incredible amount of energy and this energy is not usually used constructively. Many teams use meeting after meeting to discuss problems and the deplorable state of affairs and to list the shortcomings – but a step in the direction of the goal is taken only hesitantly. How much energy is dissipated in this way? How much efficiency is lost? The art of leading or participating in a team is to focus these energies and use them for shaping a future together. **A team is not a problem that needs to be analysed and solved but a potential to be unfolded.**

Opportunities in Turbulent Team Situations

The way in which people work together, communicate and exchange ideas is an essential contributory factor to the success of companies and organisations. Teams play a crucial role here and are therefore in an exposed position: often they are confronted with central and tricky tasks. The management has high expectations regarding the efficiency of project teams and departments. Leading a team under this kind of pressure is no simple task. You have to think of many things at the same time, and, additionally, team dynamics are often unpredictable. Turbulence in teams is more prevalent than you would want it to be, especially in hectic times.

Life **is** change. Since a dynamic, lively team changes continuously, difficult situations are the rule rather than the exception. Therefore, it is less important for the team to avoid such conflicts. What is important is to be able to deal with these situations in the daily life of the team, or to use them as a starting point for further development. In the SolutionCircle, tension and conflict are seen as stepping-stones for new development. Therefore, it is not simply about 'managing conflict' or 'solving problems'. The solution- and resource- oriented method opens up the possibility of using tension in the team to develop the team. Turbulence is seen as a positive sign of life. A turbulent situation in the team can always provide a starting point for a step into the future for the whole team.

Here are some examples of situations in which the SolutionCircle can be used:

- A team would like to grow together, improve the integration of new members and improve performance.
- Tension has grown between individual members of a team and this makes communication among team members extremely difficult. The team would like to develop a new culture of collaboration.
- The nine members of a management board would like to develop an integrated leadership culture. There is tension due to their different expectations of each other.
- An IT project team is regularly confronted with the same kind of problems.
- An insurance company would like to resolve the conflicts between the sales force and the administration and to optimise processes.
- Collaboration between nurses and doctors in a hospital is deplorable.

- A team of teachers would like to optimise their meeting culture.

I could add to this list ad infinitum. Since the SolutionCircle is not a fixed method but consists of different elements which can be deployed individually or in any suitable sequence, there are many situations in the daily life of a team which can be dealt with more efficiently and in a more lively fashion by using the SolutionCircle. You can use the elements of the SolutionCircle for team meetings, project meetings, meetings with customers and reviews to get to sustainable solutions. The common factor in all of these contexts is that people would like to create a better future for themselves in a joint effort and would like to work towards something rather than wanting to get away from something.

Working with the SolutionCircle in hectic team situations has several advantages:

- By exploring past experiences of success you attain a more positive picture of yourselves. Ah-ha experiences emerge: 'Oh, actually, we are not as bad as we thought!'
- The potential of the team and how it can be used in the future becomes very clear. New images emerge about what this team can yet become. A vision develops which is built on the resources of the team.
- The method creates trust and removes the fear of being embarrassed, criticised or judged.
- The goals and plans for the future developed by the team are based on the resources in the team. The team members gain more confidence in the possibility that the measures agreed upon can actually be carried out since they have experienced elements of them in the past. Thus the likelihood of actually carrying out agreed steps increases.

- Time and energy are concentrated on developing a solution and carrying it out. This saves time.
- We become stronger as we work on our strengths. This is very motivating for the participants, and they enjoy it. They can be seen livening up and remaining active.
- By concentrating on existing resources, the identity of the team is strengthened. The team members are more satisfied with their work and their willingness to perform also increases. It is often forgotten that the environment can enable and foster collective and individual learning.
- It also becomes clear that not everything has to be changed. A lot is already functioning well and should be kept that way. The good things that happened in the past deserve to be recognised and celebrated.

Working in the Performance – Learning – Enjoyment Triangle

If you are leading a team, you want to do this successfully. Everybody wants to be successful. Sometimes this is said explicitly, sometimes it is implicitly assumed. Success, however, has very different faces. Ask your employees – you will get very diverse answers: money, satisfaction, achieving goals, finishing projects, having fun, enhancing reputation etc. Everybody in the team wants to be successful, but very seldom do we speak about our understanding of what success would look like.

From the viewpoint of the company, success will always be attached to the financial success of the company. The team is measured by its contribution to performance. Financial success is part of the framework that cannot be negotiated. Good teamwork is nothing without it. The team exists to carry out an order or to perform a task.

What is 'successful teamwork' for the SolutionCircle? The performance of the team is only one factor in it. Tim Gallwey describes two other factors influencing performance in his book 'The Inner Game of Work'. 'Enjoying work' and 'Learning at work' influence performance and vice versa. **Without learning at work and without enjoyment, performance suffers.** Nevertheless, managers often feel threatened when performance is decreasing and respond by exerting more pressure to get more results. And so the opportunity for enjoyment and learning decreases. The resulting vicious circle hinders the whole potential for performance.

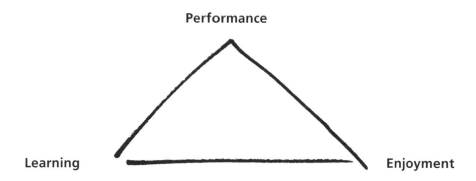

The Seminar of Daily Life

In the long run, a team can only be successful if every team member has the opportunity to learn and discover new things at work and can broaden his or her competencies in day-to-day work life. In the past, we used the knowledge and skills that were already there in order to achieve profitable results. Today we see work as a process in which you can develop your abilities while producing results, in order to be able to reach even better results in the future. If teams use every opportunity to learn and evolve, top performance is ensured. The needs of customers, the situation of the market, company strategy or the competition's products change incredibly quickly. Only if a team can move elegantly and agilely in this changing environment, can it perform at the necessary level.

Daily life offers the best opportunities to learn: the customer can teach us how to sell, the employee can teach us how to lead, my colleague can teach cooperation. No seminar can be as effective as daily work life when it comes to providing a demanding yet supportive learning environment. The 'seminar of daily life' has open doors, and everybody can choose to participate in it or to leave after a while. The seminar waits patiently for our return and allows us the freedom to choose whether we want to be aware or unaware, perceptive or dull, whether we want to learn or not. In order to be able to survive in our fast-lived times, willingness to learn is very important for the individual as well as for the whole team.

This is the reason why learning plays a central role in working with the SolutionCircle. However, this is not classical school learning where what is often most important is getting rid of mistakes. By contrast, we are trying to increase successes. Successes are analysed for factors that had a positive influence on the current results. This new found knowledge is then transferred to the situation at hand and this makes it is possible to achieve excellent results in fast changing situations. Neither theories nor models – but individual team members' reflections on their daily experience – form the centre of this learning.

Enjoying Work

It seems to be quite common to think that work cannot be enjoyable (or at least not much). Some people even say that nowadays work automatically equals stress and exhaustion. If you do not over-exert yourself, you are not taking your work seriously enough. So, it is not surprising that most people, if they were given a choice, would prefer a vacation to work. On vacation, life is carefree, fun, without responsibility, whereas work is seen as drudgery.

We do feel something when we are at work: our feelings oscillate between misery and pleasure; we sense something between total emptiness and absolute fulfillment. We are somewhere on that scale. The question is where are we and where are we heading?

Most people know from their own experience that they work better when they like working. 'Job satisfaction' directly influences performance and learning. Admittedly, it is not always easy to enjoy being at work: maybe one problem arises after the other; people that we rely on may let us down; we can lose money; the market can break down; maybe the bosses of our companies are terrible people. The list of things that can rob us of fulfillment at work seems endless.

One crucial factor in keeping work enjoyable is the relationships among the team members. If communication in the team is based on appreciation, honesty and trust, this will contribute to the well-being and performance of every single team member.

The three elements, performance, learning and enjoyment influence one another. A team is successful when these three elements are in balance and support each other constructively. However, this balance is not static: wherever people are collaborating, you will have problems and conflicts. The triangle of performance, learning and enjoyment can become unbalanced. This can happen every day, and is therefore the norm rather than the exception. The question for a successful team is therefore: how well are we able to re-establish the balance. This is where the SolutionsCircle can help.

Teams are not Machines

Leading a team means steering a complex system, which is truly not easy. Companies, associations, teams, families – all these are highly complex systems that have one thing in common. None of them can be controlled or influenced linearly, one-sidedly, or in a straight goal-oriented fashion. They are not machines that function in a foreseeable way, that work at the push of a button and that can be repaired in a shop when broken. Wherever people are involved, where people live and work together, many single elements mutually influence one another. Every one of our actions – be it as a team leader or as a team member – is a 'shot in the dark'. We cannot predict how a person is going to react to a question, a threat or a request of ours – and if we ask different people the reaction is going to be different every time.

In her book 'Beratung ohne Ratschlag' (Consulting without Advice), Sonja Radatz explains very appropriately:

> Whatever we do or don't do, has consequences – we just don't know what they are. For example, we can assume that the announcement 'next year we will have to double turnover!' will cause an active change. What is so devilish about it is that we never know in advance what the change will be. We are dealing with non-trivial living beings ..., thinking, feeling human beings who respond in any way imaginable and can decide anew on how to react and respond every moment of their lives. (p. 42)

As a team leader, you can influence a team – you can ask a question, order something, pass on information, etc. But you cannot cause anyone to react exactly the way that you would want them to. Nevertheless, you can do quite a bit to ensure that the reaction of the individual team members goes towards a common direction.

Creating the Right Conditions

One of the central tasks of managers is creating a framework and conditions that enable their employees to work optimally. Creating this framework is an ongoing process and does not consist of a single action that is completed once and for all. It is important to check the results continuously, see whether it comes closer to the goal, vary the conditions and reflect on the effect once again.

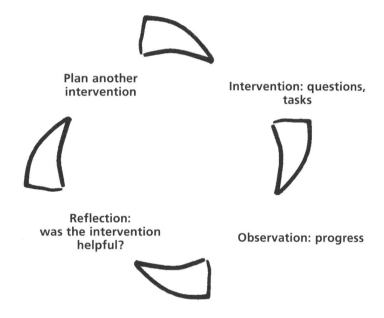

Plan another intervention

Intervention: questions, tasks

Reflection: was the intervention helpful?

Observation: progress

You do something (intervention), observe the consequences, and reflect on the results (what worked?). Depending on these results, you do something again – it is a continuous circle that follows the rule: **if what you are doing is creating good results, do more of it.**

The same principle applies when you are using the SolutionCircle in your daily work life. Since you cannot change your team at the push of a button, it is important to test your interventions continuously and see whether they are useful. That means that you do more of what yields good results and change what is not working. Working with the SolutionCircle requires a personal process of reflection, which, in turn, helps you with your work because you can learn more about your leadership qualities. You can find out which kinds of questions and statements or which way of passing on information help you to add a valuable contribution to the team's joint success.

> **What is the SolutionCircle?**
> *Solution* stands for a clear orientation towards solutions and resources. Working with the SolutionCircle, we use time and energy to develop powerful and dynamic solutions that are customised to the given situation. We aim at identifying the existing skills and strengths in order to focus on them and to reinforce them.
>
> *Circle* describes the circle that expresses the movement of continuous optimisation of the interventions (questions, appreciative feedback, listening, an observation task, etc.) oriented at achieving the goal.

Leading by Questions

If you as manager decide to use elements of the SolutionCircle, you will deploy ideas used in professional coaching. You will discover and develop a leadership style of coaching. This is why we call the person who leads a workshop as facilitator 'coach'. The most important tools in coaching are questions, and you lead through a SolutionCircle mainly by asking questions: questions that aim at developing a solution and that develop the team. If the conditions for working with a SolutionCircle are in place, the main task of the coach is to see to it that these conditions are maintained and that the participants can work as effectively as possible in the direction of the goals decided upon.

As coach, you are not the expert, the person who already knows everything and is sure of the correct solution. You are more of a companion who by sharing his or her knowledge helps the team to avoid running in wrong directions or getting stuck in dead ends. **The coach is competent in leading the workshop, while the participants of the team are competent in developing the solution.**

Different managers, who are already working intensively with the SolutionCircle, report that this is not always an easy role to take. Sometimes one's own ideas get in the way. However, they also say that it is very relaxing not to have to produce the best solution for everyone all the time. Their experience shows that this method helps them to feel secure and calm especially in turbulent situations when they concentrate on guiding the process. And in addition, a coaching leadership style helps the employees to become more independent and responsible in the long run.

As a coach, you are an attentive companion who makes the development of new knowledge possible by posing solution-oriented questions. Your team can thus discover new possibilities, develop innovative approaches for solutions and test new methods – and all of that with a constant eye on the goal that you want to achieve together. This only happens if employees can optimally contribute their experience and competence. They do not receive prefabricated orders but are asked for their own suggestions for solutions. This way, they become responsible for the development process. Moreover, **this is how you develop new, customised solutions.** Solutions – and this is very important – that are owned and agreed on by everybody. We do not need just any solution, but we need the one solution fitting for **this** team in **this** situation. Tailor-made or customised solutions can develop if all participants can work on them together.

If there is a price to be paid for this method, it is the patience that you have to have and the fact that your employees will develop in part independently of your own knowledge. Nevertheless, even this is a chance for comprehensive development rather than anything else.

Some managers are afraid of having to concentrate primarily on asking questions and thereby having to give up some of the responsibility for developing the solution. They are afraid of becoming superfluous or losing power and respect. Managers generally assume that the company, as well as the employees, expect the manager to design and prescribe solutions. There are two very important facts in this context:

a) The method of leading a conversation that is described here is an additional skill that you can use as one of your leadership tools – however, it does not replace other tasks that you have to fulfill as a leader. You will continue to have to set goals and define frameworks, pass on your professional expertise and thereby add to the expertise of your team members. You will also still have to take control sometimes and still have to take decisions for the team and – last but not least – you will not be able to avoid having to issue unpleasant instructions and orders. However, as a valuable addition to your other leadership skills, you will find various tools here, which have proven very useful and efficient in numerous situations.

b) Some managers also tell me that they do not use a coaching style of leadership since they are afraid that their employees will no longer acknowledge their professional skill and knowledge and that they will thereby lose authority. This fear can only be counteracted if you manage to establish the competencies that a coaching style of leadership demands as a key qualification. Limiting leadership to asking solution-oriented questions and guiding the process is an extra-ordinary leadership skill: it is a leadership skill that is used when you are aiming at the long-term development of responsibility and at the creation of a sustainable development processes in the team.

Leave Problems Where They Are

It is important to leave problems where they arise. Managers, especially, are in danger of feeling responsible for various issues that really belong in the team or between individual team members. As a coach working with the SolutionCircle, your task is clear. You support the solution by contributing to the process through posing solution-oriented questions to all involved. Thus, you are responsible for the process and not for the problems. You are relieved of the task of having to produce new ideas for solving a problem continuously – and, in addition, the real glory for the solution stays with your employees, who actually found the solution. This way you strengthen the confidence and self-image of your employees.

When working with the SolutionCircle, you as manager are asked to hold back a bit. In this way, you enable your employees to contribute their skill and knowledge to the development of a customised solution. It is important to encourage them to formulate their personal evaluations and ideas. Finally, yet importantly, they start to take over entrepreneurial responsibility – and is this not exactly what you wish for as a team leader or head of department?

2 Four Basic Principles

'Problem talk creates problems. Solution talk creates solutions.'

Steve de Shazer

Crisis in an IT Team: Part One

Anna, manager of a small IT support department in a telecommunications company, felt helpless and at a loss what to do. She had been sensing that things were not running smoothly in the team for weeks, and at the last team meeting, conflict finally broke out. When she introduced the new strategy that she wanted to present to higher management, the discussion became very heated. Some team members would have liked to be involved in working on the strategy much earlier since they had fundamentally different ideas on certain central aspects. Others in the team felt that they were only given the boring work and that this would not change in the future. Two team members who were obviously not getting along at all had hardly spoken to one another for a while. Now at the team meeting, these two started arguing about every little detail. Anna knew that all eight members of her team were under a lot of pressure and in addition to that, a projected reorganisation had produced a lot of insecurity since it was not known whether there would be lay-offs. Therefore, dissatisfaction of the employees had increased over the previous weeks. This had not gone unnoticed by their internal customers who had detected flaws in the handling of a couple of jobs.

Anna was pleased that she had been able to stay calm in the meeting and that her suggestion to take a morning together in order to deal with the internal tension was taken up quickly, with everybody hoping for a change to the better.

This was no simple task for the manager of the department since a lot of tension seemed to have piled up. Moreover, which topics had to be worked on now: was it collaboration, the performance of the team, the new strategy, dealing constructively with the latest reorganisation? Often we do not have a clear-cut and unambiguous problem in a team but various problems that influence one another. How can you deal with the dynamics in the team without ending up with the team in shambles? Anna decided to faciliate this workshop herself and not to hire an external coach or consultant. She would be able to do that later if need be.

The Workshop: Part 1

After a short introduction to the agenda that Anna proposed for the workshop, she started like this:

'I would like to start with a little exercise. I am aware of the fact that this is a pretty demanding exercise needing a lot of imagination. My experience with this team has been that it has always been possible to deal with new situations and master them imaginatively. What do you think, would you like to do this exercise even though it seems a bit unusual at first?'

After the team had agreed she went on:

'Please answer the following questions and note the answers on a flipchart:

a)   *If our team were able to solve the problems and conflicts at hand really well and could turn into a true "superteam" – what would this team look like in two years time?*

  – What would you notice that told you that everything is working well in the team?

  – What would our colleagues and customers be saying about us?

– What exactly would each of us be doing differently?

b) *On a scale of 1 to 10, how high is your motivation to spend energy and time taking the first steps in the direction of "superteam"?*

The team members were a bit surprised by this kind of task since they had expected to get ample opportunities to complain. Nevertheless, they overcame their initial resistance quickly and started describing their ideas for the future.

After less than an hour they could tell each other about a desirable future. They talked about retaining everybody in the team. There would be fun and laughter again. They would have structured their service clearly, modified the procedures. They developed clear ideas on how they would lead their regular team meetings and were discussing a new form of meetings on employee qualification.

Their ideas about the future were very realistic and oriented at possible implementation.

Focusing on Solutions

Anna had dared to do something courageous. Without a thorough analysis of the problem, she had asked what the situation would look like if it was satisfactory for everybody. In this way, she led her team directly to the level of solutions. This brings us to the first of the four principles of the SolutionCircle:

We use the available energy and time solely for exploring solutions.

Instead of trying to find out more about problems and difficulties, we jump directly to the level of solutions and work on concrete images of the solution.

From the Level of Problems to the Level of Solutions

At the level of solutions, we are talking about a future that every-body wants. The team constructs a new reality which is so attractive that it frees their energy. By exchanging ideas about a desirable future, the team creates a concentrated and constructive atmos-phere. Goals become tangible by describing observable behaviour in the future. It is crucial to find as much detailed information as possible about what successful actions in the future would look like and what the consequences of these actions would be for other people.

Maybe you have already realised the following: the more we talk about conflicts, the bigger and more complex they become. The same is true for solutions: the more we find out about the solution, the more conscious we become about what life would be like if our problem were solved and the greater our desire to reach this state. Simply wishing for a better situation together, imagining a concrete better future, in which we would like to work and live, frees the energy to work sustainably for that future in the team.

The future can be created. Everyone can help shape the future by his or her actions. Or, as Insoo Kim Berg, one of the co-founders of the solution-focused approach, said: 'The future is not a slave to past

Level of solutions

Level of problems

events. Every team and every individual can therefore find many useful steps, which will make a more satisfactory life highly probable.'

The step taken here by the manager of the department is called 'Future Perfect'[1] in the SolutionCircle. Only when a team has a clear picture of which direction the desired changes should take can it start taking first steps. It is therefore very sensible to spend a lot of time finding out exactly what the desired future beyond the problem should look like.

Words Create Reality

Our perception of reality is shaped and influenced by language. In every company and in every team, people are constantly creating an image of their organisation that describes what it was like before, what it is like now, and what it could be like. Naturally, every member of the organisation has his or her own view – nevertheless, there is a joint image that is supported by a majority and is communicated day by day in their stories. People constantly tell stories – in the cafeteria, in the hallways, in e-mails, before and after meetings. They may be long or short and sometimes they may only consist of a joke or a key phrase. Telling stories is one of the ways in which we structure reality and give meaning to our experience.

The dominant stories of a team are the expression of the perceptions of its members. They are not reality but the lenses through which reality is observed. The stories that people tell in organisations can be inspiring or polluting the atmosphere. We all know this from personal experience: we love to indulge ourselves by telling negative or 'sour' stories, making them bigger, embellishing them. Especially in teams, the repertoire of veritable 'horror stories' can be very large. However, if the negative stories predominate, we start perceiving the organisation or the team as a big heap of junk and stop seeing the existing resources and potential.

[1] I first came across this term in the book by Jackson and McKergow (2002).

What is so disastrous about this is that we turn into the picture that we make of ourselves. We become the stories that we tell about ourselves. Aspects we focus our attention on get bigger. There are innumerable examples of this. G.B. Shaw's story Pygmalion, the basis for the world famous musical My Fair Lady, gave its name to the Pygmalion effect. There are several studies that show that students produce exactly the quality of results that the teachers expect of them. The teacher's expectation is subliminally transferred to the students and shapes the image that they make of themselves. And then they turn into that image. Historians have shown that great cultures start blooming when they create a positive image of themselves and their future – and that these cultures start to decay when this image loses its power.

A lively, successful team has a positive, dynamic self-image. A negative self-image makes every development practically impossible. This is why we as leaders have to contribute to the development of a powerful image of the future in conversations.

Team leaders can contribute a lot to solution-oriented conversation, especially by the way they lead team meetings. The way a meeting or conversation is conducted influences how effective and helpful it is in shaping the future. Conversations that help find out and determine what kind of team work the members would like to have, which kind of balance between learning, performance and enjoyment is important for the team, and which actions bring the team closer to this desired outcome are much more helpful than other conversations.

A team starts shaping its future by sitting together and exchanging promising ideas. The framework is canvassed and new images are created together. In the exchange the team produces stories about the future that show how it can be created together. Of course, individual suggestions are tested for the likelihood of their implementation and also measured against the conditions in the environment. The future perfect is not used to develop unrealistic or utopian goals. Moreover, in the future perfect we create space to think through different scenarios. This way, the team members are given the opportunity to actively create a future that they would like to belong to themselves.

Finding Solutions rather than Solving Problems

How can managers encourage more helpful conversations in the team? One of the things they can do is focusing on 'finding solutions' rather than on 'solving problems'. At first glance, this does not seem like a very meaningful distinction: finding solutions instead of solving problems. However, in daily life this is the difference that makes a difference! When something goes wrong or is not working, we usually ask:

- Why did it not work out as intended?
- What were the causes of the failure?
- What did we do wrong?

In working with the SolutionCircle, we concentrate on the future – because the future can be shaped by us!

- How should it be?
- What would be the boldest idea in this situation?
- What do we need to achieve this?

Most people are used to analysing problems and then solving the problem according to the diagnosis. The SolutionCircle uses the time available to find out as much as possible about goals and approaches to the solution. Instead of asking analytical questions about the past, we lead a conversation that produces a detailed image of what the goal would look like:

No analytical questions about the past ...	... but questions about shaping the future
How did the problem arise?	What do you need in order to solve this problem successfully?
Who caused the problem?	When a miracle happens, and all your problems are solved satisfactorily, what exactly will be different then?
Why did he do that?	How could he behave differently in the future?
What is the worst aspect of this issue?	What exactly should be different in the future?
Why?	What behaviour would indicate to other people that you have reached your goal?

In the daily life of a manager, this change in perspective from a problem treating stance to one of developing solutions can have great effects and can free up blocked situations.

The headmaster of a school for children with special learning needs once told me a memorable example of what solution building questions can achieve in normal leadership situations: he had participated in a two day seminar on solution-oriented leadership and went home with the task of experimenting with the new ideas and models. After three weeks, the group met again for a reflecting day. The headmaster told us about an important success in his work.

For over a year, he as the headmaster and his team of teachers had been having a lot of difficulties with the weekly team meetings. Up to that point they had had a two and a half hour pedagogical conference every week plus an additional compulsory organisational meeting on another day of the week. All in all, they had been having three and a half hours of team meetings every week! In spite of the time involved, they were all very unhappy with the results because they could not find time for all the topics on the agenda. Even though the meetings were often longer than anticipated, not everything that was important to the individual team members could be discussed. On the contrary, the team members felt like they were under constant time pressure and were criticising the facilitator of the meeting for this. They had already started several initiatives to deal with this unsatisfactory state, had looked for causes and had talked about it amongst themselves.

The headmaster now thought about how he could approach this problem in a solution focused way.

At the end of the next meeting, he passed out a piece of paper with three questions that every teacher was to answer:

a) *If you could design a meeting in which you would like to partici-pate actively, what would it look like?*

b) *What exactly would you be doing differently?*

c) *Were there any situations in recent meetings that were a bit similar to what you imagine? What exactly was happening then?*

The headmaster evaluated this survey and designed a meeting structure based on the answers that made it possible to deal with the pedagogical as well as with the organisational part within two and a half hours.

His explanation was: 'I am not quite sure, but I think that by asking about a desirable future, it was possible for everybody to think in a new frame of reference and let go of old useless frames. Instead of voicing new reproaches and pointing out obstacles, we were able to develop new ideas. In our previous attempts to solve our meeting problem, we had started on the level of the problem. We were asking what was going wrong and why. This resulted in a strange problem spiral that pulled us downwards, deeper and deeper into the problem. These conversations often ended in mutual reproach. All of us were rather helpless, and this helplessness increased the size of our block.'

The Level of Problems

When we are working on the level of problems, we deal with deficits, look for culprits and find explanations why this or that cannot be implemented anyway. Bosses, another department – generally other people – are the reason that I am not feeling good and that I cannot fulfill my job as successfully as I would like to. Teams can waste a lot of time and energy supporting the members in their respective discontent – not only in team meetings but also in conversations during the breaks. Sometimes you feel helpless at the mercy of the unfortunate situation. Especially in conflict situations, you can have a 'problem spiral', which actually draws a team deeper and deeper into the pit until there is almost no hope for improvement.

What is surprising is that a team can sometimes even forge its identity by adhering to the problem focus. If the environment is so incompetent, the company does not have a well designed strategy, and nothing is done for the job satisfaction of the employees – in the opinion of this team, anyway – it is very easy to distinguish between outside (the incompetents) and inside (it is quite astonishing that we can yield such good results in light of all this). This view can lead to the team members building a kind of fatalistic community. Teams that construct their identity from the deplorable situation often lack the energy to initiate change or to take the future actively into their own hands. If we meet this kind of situation, we have to establish an image or vision of the future that is very strong and that contains everything that the team members cherish about their current situation for change to be possible at all.

Leaving out Analysis of the Problem

Understanding exactly what the problem is plays only a very minor role in working on concrete solutions with the SolutionCircle. We are convinced that solutions based on concrete visions of a goal and on the resources of the team can be implemented more effectively than solutions that rest on the analysis of mistakes and deficits.

When you are dealing with conflict, it can be important for the team to talk about problems. However, in this context it is not the analysis that is central but the exchange of individual perceptions that need to be voiced. This kind of conversation can be helpful for the development of a solution since individual team members need to talk about the difficulties in order to gain some distance from the problem. Such conversations are sometimes necessary to make talking about solutions possible at all. Sometimes it is also necessary to vent frustrations, hurts and sadness to free one's thinking and feelings for a change process. To speak about difficulties can be helpful, then. Therefore, it is very important to deal respectfully, carefully and appreciatively to descriptions of the problem. Under no circumstances should the problem be labeled unimportant or talked about in a deprecatory manner.

Building on Success

Crisis in an IT Team: Part 2 of the Workshop

As a second step in the workshop, the manager of the department asked the individual team members to place themselves on a scale of 1 to 10. 10 was the desirable future, 1 the absolute opposite of that. They positioned their view of the situation between 2 and 5 at most. Anna did not show much interest in the deficit, the gap between 2 or 5 and 10 but focused on what was already working. She asked: 'What are we doing that gets us to 2 (or 5)? We could be much lower, but you say we are already at 2 (or 5). What is it that we are doing pretty well, then?'

Harbingers of a Solution

Here the manager introduces the element of scales. This instrument makes it possible for us to find out what is already working. It is the second basic principle of the SolutionCircle: we do not orient ourselves to what went wrong. We do not analyse the gap between yesterday and tomorrow, but we look for everything we can identify as small glimpses into a desirable future. These signs provide very useful hints at how we can proceed in our change process. By asking: 'In the last months, have there been any highlights, when the problem or the conflict was absent or did not show up as violently?' we uncover and illuminate successful possibilities for action. In addition, the confidence that something actually can be done to bring about change rises – we show that it has already happened at least once in the past.

If we turn back in the SolutionCircle and look at the past, we try to find situations in which something of the desired state in the future has already surfaced. We reflect on what worked and try to find out which personal traits or actions led to it. Focusing on the exceptions to the problematic situation usually reveals obvious (partial) solutions.

In this IT team workshop, one team member complained that his colleagues were not taking him seriously, which was why he had almost stopped contact with one of them in particular. His contributions in project meetings were regularly ignored. Therefore, he had fallen silent and had stopped showing any initiative. This team member put himself at a 2 on the scale in comparison to the future perfect at 10. When the manager asked about situations in which there had been a real exchange with his colleagues – in the SolutionCircle we call these great moments 'highlights' – he mentioned a few informal conversations in which he had felt taken seriously. It is important to have a very good look at this small highlight and focus on the solution: 'What exactly was different in these informal conversations? How exactly did you behave differently in these informal conversations? What are you saying, exactly?' These findings can provide information on how to transfer this successful behaviour to the general meeting culture.

The Power of Orienting towards Resources

We can always look at the past from different angles. If you asked twenty people to analyse a certain team (or an organisation) without giving them any further instructions, they would probably come back with a long list mainly describing weaknesses. Looking for deficits seems an almost automatic mechanism, which is deeply rooted in classical organisation and team development. Consultants come up with diagnoses by leading different workshops, interviews or by observation, and these diagnoses are then presented to those concerned. The deficits are often labeled 'new opportunities', but most of the time they still cause resistance in the participants: 'Actually, it is not that bad', people say – and right then, you can see the opponents of the change process forming. If you proceed in a deficit-oriented fashion, it is all too easy to rouse a defensive attitude in the participants. They start trying to find culprits and blame for the miserable situation is passed around.

The need to work on deficits is often overestimated. Even in strategy development processes, where strengths/weaknesses analyses are a standard procedure, it is less important to know one's weaknesses in comparison to the competition. It is far more important to know one's own unique points and to discover opportunities and use them. If you know these factors well, you will find the right direction without a detailed knowledge of your weaknesses.

Dealing with our weaknesses makes us weaker. Knowing about our strengths makes us stronger. This is why in the SolutionCircle we are interested in what has already worked well. We are looking for incidents, highlights, in which small or larger successes emerged. Who did what exactly and what was different about this situation? The SolutionCircle wants to uncover what has worked well before. We learn from these discoveries and base developments on them.

We construct the change processes on the basis of the successes of the team rather than its deficits.

In working with teams, it is time and again fascinating to see what happens when the team members realise that the workshop is not about talking about deficits, weaknesses, or who is to blame but about finding out what went well in the past and learning from that. Tense facial muscles relax, eyes come alive and suddenly you feel a new energy in the room. You will notice it yourself: it is a very different way of working. Although it seems hard and tough at first, once you make the effort, you get lively discussions, and energy and motivation take the place of lack of interest and half-heartedness.

If something does not work, do something different!

This is the second part of the principle of building on success. Clear, unequivocal, and reasonable – however, still very far from being implemented in the every day work life. I often come across the opposite: if something does not work, people try and make it work by using the exact same measures and methods. They do 'more of the same': they try harder, intensify their efforts and over-exert themselves. One manager of a department told me that he had been trying to get a grip on his 'time management' for years. Since he always felt stressed out and he was constantly up to his neck in unfinished tasks, he had already been to different seminars and tried out different time management systems. He had a very structured approach to his task, differentiated between important and urgent, classified into A-, B- and C-tasks ... but he still did not see his pile of to-do tasks getting smaller. Sometimes this problem even followed him into his dreams. As a consequence, he assumed that he still did not have his time system under control. He used more time for planning, drew up even more exact plans, and filled in his 'to-do' list meticulously. But the more he concentrated on the tasks that still needed to be done, the less he succeeded in getting them done in time and well enough to satisfy him. He constantly exerted himself and his willpower and became increasingly desperate.

This manager tried to solve his problem by doing 'more of the same', by intensifying the same strategy, and following it more consistently as if adhering to the motto: 'If at first you don't succeed, try, try, try again.'

Sometimes the solution to the problem can become a problem itself – a kind of vicious circle that we need to break out of. Experience shows that a vicious circle can be broken by attempts at a solution that look paradoxical at first. Attempts to break the circle seem absurd, unexpected, or irrational. They are often essentially surprising.

For example, what helped the above manager was to go home from work half an hour early on three days of the week. He wanted to use these 30 minutes to do something that he had not done in a while that had nothing to do with work. Most of the time, he simply tended his garden. Sometimes he went out for a drink or quietly read the newspaper. This half hour slowly turned into a kind of 'sacred time' that became more and more precious to him and that he wanted to defend against his unaccomplished tasks. He did not attend yet another time management seminar, but he began to reject tasks that he would previously have accepted. He also started ending meetings earlier to be able to get off work sooner. He still planned his time very meticulously – but he had another goal: he wanted to keep up his 'sacred half hour'!

In order to break up blocked situations, we often have to do something very different and have to leave our well-trodden paths. However, it is still necessary to distinguish carefully between interventions that work and those that will lead into another dead end.

I sometimes still fall into that trap and build my own vicious circle of solutions that do not work and then try to get to my goal by using more energy and enthusiasm instead of changing the method of the intervention.

For instance, I was leading a project team that was to plan a crucial change in the hierarchical structure of a company in order to achieve closer contact with the customers and increase overall quality. At the end of the second workshop, there were a few things that needed to be done. Flipcharts needed to be prepared, arrangements made for the next meeting etc. When I wanted to allocate the tasks, there was silence – nobody at that moment had time to do it. In the end, I was left to do almost everything. Afterwards, I thought that I probably had not clarified the roles enough and had not adequately pointed out that everybody was responsible for contributing. When I made up for that by explaining about responsibility at the next meeting, even less happened. The more pressure I exerted and the more I pointed to the rules and the project contract, the more passive the team members became. I once even got the manager responsible for the whole project to talk to the team to help them realise that the project team also has to carry their share of the burden. However, this, too, was 'more of the same': reproaches and pressure did not help – no matter which form they took.

The solution for this difficulty was rather surprising. Once I had to cancel my participation in a meeting on short notice, and so I asked someone else to lead it for me on that occasion. I felt very bad about not being present at the meeting since I was the project leader. However, my absence led to the project team dealing with the new situation a little helplessly at first, but very creatively in the end. They developed a totally new quality assurance model and presented it to me in the next session. I was thrilled with the stronger commitment of the team and asked how it had become possible so suddenly. What it all boiled down to was that they had felt responsible for the meeting, that they could choose the working method themselves, and that they were free to choose which points on the agenda they would cover – they could work on the topics that were really important to them. We tried integrating these points into future meetings, and from then on, there was an almost tangible rise in energy and commitment in the team. Often a small change in your behaviour can cause great changes in the system.

Illuminating Resources

Traditional methods of working with teams assume that crises and problems arise because a department or a team is incapable of dealing with a situation adequately. The team lacks certain competencies or it is not flexible enough. **Working with the SolutionCircle, we assume that all skills necessary to master a turbulent situation are already present in the team.** As a coach, your task is to support the team in the (re)discovery of these forgotten resources. You create a framework in which the existing resources can stand out more. In this context, what we mean by resources is every available tool and every available skill that can be used for developing a solution. Commitment, motivation, loyalty to the company, friendliness, or experience can all be resources – as well as tangible tools like time, money, means of communicating, or professional skills. Even things that seem negative at first can be used positively for developing a solution. For instance being hard-headed can point to the ability to defend one's opinion with a lot of energy; and customers' complaints can be seen as special service requests or opportunities to improve the product.

Recognising these resources and becoming conscious of their value in reaching your goal is difficult. Working with scales, like our manager of the IT specialists, can be very helpful here. Simple questions like: 'What did you contribute to help us get to a 2?' or 'Which of your abilities helped you to react in this way?' make resources visible. A change process can be carried out much more effectively on the basis of personal resources because you increase confidence this way. By illuminating the existing resources, the team members are actively confirmed in their strengths. **It is not about covering deficits but about illuminating existing skills and strengths and using them for the development of a solution.**

There are many advantages to concentrating on existing strengths again and again:

- However large and intractable turbulence in a team, every team member has strengths that can be systematised and used to improve the quality of its work. In our experience, changes that are based on existing strengths are also much easier to implement than those that aim at reducing deficits.
- Motivation of the participants is also increased by talking about each other's strengths.
- Discovering and naming resources can best be done in conversation with everybody involved. The coach does not know what is best for the participants to work on a suitable solution; but the participants can discover a customised solution that they can implement themselves.
- Additionally, illuminating resources makes it easier for the facilitator of the process to avoid the temptation to judge or criticise the team or individual team members for their difficulties. In fact, it leads to an attitude of discovering with amazement how the participants succeed in mastering their job even under difficult circumstances.

The manager of a research and development department had booked me as an external team coach. He had taken over the department almost a year ago and was increasingly confronted with criticism with regard to his lead-

ership style. The Human Resources department had already contacted him and had carefully asked whether he would possibly be interested in further leadership training. The team members were used to achieving results very quickly under high pressure and to initiating and carrying out projects for new products. They felt that the new manager did not sell the developments well enough to the top management, which led to cuts in the budgets. Product developments therefore had to be stopped half way. In addition, he delayed projects by not making decisions or by making them too slowly.

When we were looking at resources in one of the first workshops, some very interesting discoveries were made. The manager was ascribed skills like high professional competence, scrupulous conceptualising and a thorough and detailed way of working. Additionally, he was described as extremely precise, discriminating and honest, always aiming at producing high quality work and eliminating all risks. The team members saw their own resources differently. They were fast, sometimes too fast in their actions (others were often surprised at how quickly you could get results from this department) – and were happy with an 80% solution. They often could come up with a solution without writing a concept first or doing solid research. They were very communicative and were able to inspire enthusiasm in others for their ideas. Sometimes, they exerted themselves way over their limits for their projects.

When it became clear in the course of the workshop that we had a set of very different resources at hand, a large part of the team turbulence cleared up. These differences could lead to conflicts but they could also supplement one another very nicely. Nobody had intentionally done anything wrong and nobody needed any additional competencies at the moment. It was a matter of planning together how to utilise their different resources to best effect. Should a member of the team accompany the manager to presentations? How could the precise thinking and detailed conceptualising of the manager be integrated into product development?

With these questions, team development was the centre of attention, not mutual reproach and disappointment. A little later, the manager could tell the Human Resources department that he did not need to attend another leadership seminar at the moment.

Crisis in an IT team: Part 3

At the end of the first morning, the team were exploring possibilities of getting a small step closer to 10. They were not looking for great leaps but for small actions in everyday life.

The goal was not to discuss a detailed action plan but to talk about different possibilities for action and what they could possibly lead to.

After this discussion, Anna decided to give a small observation task to the participants of the workshop, a bit like homework:

'Everyone is free to try out one of the possible new actions in our everyday work – each team member can implement something, or not. But there is one task that I would like to give to everybody: we will reconvene in three weeks. Choose three days in the coming three weeks in which you will watch closely to see if you can find small visible signs or harbingers of the "superteam" state that you would like to have in the future. Maybe these are only small and inconspicuous – maybe not. Write down these signs at the end of each observation day. Of course, I will do the same. We will exchange our observations in our next workshop.

In addition to that, we will decide next time which measures we would actually like to implement together in the future.'

The team manager's wrap-up seems very open and not very concrete at first glance. What can you really change by mere observation? How can observation have a positive influence on the process? How can change come about by mere observation?

What was Anna thinking when she assigned this task?

'When I was working with my team, I realised that individual team members perceived the problem differently. Some were almost offended by some things that I said, others did not mind at all. I was once again confirmed in my view that conflicts really arise in people's heads. There are no real problems – objectively, I mean – moreover, they exist for some

people and not for others. Crises are constructed by the individual team members – not intentionally or maliciously – but due to their different individual perceptions.

I was wondering whether this observation task could help to change the focus of awareness. By focusing only on what I asked them to, they would all be able to find signs of change, I hoped. If we focus on everything that is negative, we find more negative things – so it should also work the other way around.'

Anna continued: 'I was anxious and excited about the next meeting. Over the intervening period, I had noticed that the team members were reserved and careful with one another. My own presumption about the issue was about me as a woman leading an IT team. I presumed that my team members thought my technical competence was not high enough to lead them. The second meeting turned out to be a small highlight. We needed a whole hour to tell each other what we had discovered in our day to day life that could be interpreted as first glimpses of the team future. Some had written a list of what had happened – others simply gave their gut feelings. And every statement was a little bit like a small compliment to the others – most of the time not directly and formally. But everyone heard how others really appreciated even small things that they had done. I was told that two professional hints that I had given in a migration project had been really helpful. Obviously, my competence was recognised after all.

The focus had been changed once and for all. We were all able to change our frame of reference and look at ourselves and our work with different eyes. Even if our problems had not been completely solved – it is not that simple – we balanced them out with a few positive signs. This set free the energy that we needed to implement the measures that we agreed upon at the end of the second workshop. Our confidence that we would actually do it was extremely high. Everyone knew that we had already done similar things in the past. It had become clear: we can do it together!'

Finding New Perspectives

The task the team manager gave to her IT team leads us to the fourth basic principle of the SolutionCircle: by focusing awareness on something, you can find new perspectives and initiate a learning process for all involved. You can increase choices as well as the flexibility of a team. When the team leader realised that, in certain situations, her professional competence was indeed recognised, her perspective on the situation changed. Apart from being able to lead with much less stress, she also gained more confidence to voice her ideas more often in the future.

Awareness focused on one point is like shining a light on the goal that we are focusing on. We can see the goal more clearly and possibly understand it better. If we choose a wide focus, we can see the whole landscape; if it is narrow, we can see a single leaf on a tree. However, the leaf is not the tree! Our scope of understanding a situation depends on how much attention we give to the important aspects and the relationships between them. If our scope is too narrow – for example if we have 'tunnel vision' or see things in black and white – we limit our flexibility and are prone to misjudgments.

What we concentrate on also depends on our experiences and wishes. If someone is in a bad mood, he or she will undoubtedly find many reasons to get upset. No matter how hard you try, you just cannot get it right for this person. If the secretary does not feel accepted by her superior, she will find signs confirming her view every day. Harmless conversations during breaks can substantiate her suspicion. The secretary has a very narrow focus and analyses each statement of her boss to find signs that corroborate her claim. However, as human beings, we can consciously decide what to focus on. We have a choice. With each of our choices, we set priorities that determine our actions. Everybody can choose to focus consciously on certain aspects – or he or she can let momentary moods or unconscious desires choose where attention goes. Many people know this phenomenon from their school days: focused attention and concentration make it possible to learn about totally new subjects. We can learn about physics, chemistry, Latin or French. When you concentrate, you are really aware, conscious of your intention, in the here and now. It is possible to learn words of a new language or abstract formulas. This fact contains a very important realisation for team development since – just like with learning – teams develop in the direction that their attention is focused.

The secretary can choose to consciously concentrate on other aspects of collaboration with her superior, for instance on the form in which he shows appreciation, how often he says 'thank you' during the week, or maybe, how she manages to make him laugh.

By changing our focus of awareness we can gain new insights and can see – figuratively speaking – whole new parts of the landscape.

When you are working with teams, you can use an observation task to enable individual team members to gain new perspectives on an issue and start thinking in new patterns. This produces new opportunities and choices.

The Four Basic Principles

Focusing on Solutions	Talk about solutions rather than about problems.
Building on Success	If something works, do more of it.
Illuminating resources	Ask about and uncover competences and skills.
Finding new Perspectives	Change the focus of your awareness.

3 Helpful Attitudes

'Understanding does not exist. There are only more or less useful misunderstandings.'

Steve de Shazer

What is the difference between an average and a gourmet cook? Even when both are preparing the same menu and using exactly the same recipe, you will be able to detect a difference. Of course, it has something to do with experience, but what is really decisive is the attitude of the cook! The excellent cook will choose the vegetables carefully when shopping and pick the herbs fresh from the garden. He will dare to use a little bit more of this ingredient and in turn use another more sparingly. For him, cooking is an inspiration, a creative act, joyful and a bit experimental. He strives at preparing the best for his guests and wants to present them not only with a meal but with an experience.

This book is also a kind of cookbook with a simple recipe and the necessary ingredients. If you use it every day, it will work – just like a recipe in a cookbook works (even though you can still mess up the dinner). Behind the tools that you find here, behind the SolutionCircle menu, you find ideas for dealing with people, for leading people and developing and implementing the most effective solutions together. Just like the actions of a cook follow certain principles, working with the tools of the SolutionCircle follows these principles:

Experts in Customised Solutions

Consultants are often only too quick to pass on advice and hints. And managers, too, tend to construct standard solutions for their team since they have already led other teams and thus have a lot of experience. Additionally, their well-founded education helps them to find out quickly what the 'right' or 'targeted' procedure is. Consultants as well as managers like to take up the role of an 'expert' and think that they are helpful this way. In certain situations, when you are dealing with questions of gathering information or questions of organisational procedures, this can be useful and save time.

In many other situations, however, we rob the team of a great opportunity – the opportunity to find their own, customised solution and to make necessary and instructive detours.

Every turbulent team situation is unique and has implications only for the people concerned. These people are the real experts in the problem. Solutions suggested from the outside can serve as ideas here but they are not likely to fit as well as tailor-made solutions. The team has probably spent hours (days and nights) dealing with the questions. The SolutionCircle rests on the assumption that they can find the most suitable (and not just any) solution. SolutionSurfing means holding oneself and one's ideas back and opening space in which to develop a team solution.

It is not easy to hold back advice and hints, especially when you are the manager of the team. But if you are convinced that by delegating the responsibility for developing a solution, both the commitment and the initiative of your employees is strengthened and the chance for a dynamic development increases, then it becomes easier for you to take up this challenge. It simply pays back many times! Again and again, our experience is that the probability of implementing the measures agreed upon is a lot higher if the solutions have been developed by the people concerned themselves.

Productive Not-Knowing

Not-knowing means that you are impartial, it gives you permission to ask unconventional questions and leaves the responsibility for questions about the subject matter and about suitable solutions to the experts – the participants in the conflict. Not-knowing is a productive and useful prerequisite for working with the SolutionCircle. The opposite of 'not-knowing' is certainty. We generally tend to want certainty. We want to find a well-reasoned line of argument, we want to do a thorough analysis in order to find out the truth, to confirm hypotheses by clear facts and data, to work scientifically. But what seems certain to us is only our construction, our view of the world.

When working with the SolutionCircle, managers and consultants regularly report that they often start to understand what it is all about when individual team members talk about their specific professional problems. This makes managers feel a bit powerless. How can they help the individual when they do not understand much or any of what they are told? If they accept that the world is created in our heads, they will never be able to understand another person truly and fully anyway. Steering clear of trying to under-stand fully and practising 'productive not-knowing' gives them a chance of keeping out of the content. This way they can fully concentrate on their role as coach. They do not have to understand anything to be able to apply the elements of the SolutionCircle well. They can afford to be surprised and delighted about the solutions that have been produced, since they are a witness to the fact that the participants worked very hard themselves.

Not-knowing is very productive in this context. Not-knowing demonstrates respect for other opinions and new ideas. By not yielding to the temptation of certainty, it becomes possible for us to start on new paths and to be prepared for a foray into the unknown. In teams, very different opinions come together. Often they are surprising and not as you would expect as a manager. An attitude of productive not-knowing enables the coach to create a space for a discussion in which the most varied opinions can be utilised for developing a solution.

Clarity about your own Interests

Not every discussion in the team can be dealt with in a SolutionCircle – sometimes you as the responsible manager have clear interests and have to inform people of certain facts. You have made a decision that needs to be implemented. Or you have to represent and implement entrepreneurial goals. In your function as a superior, you set the framework regarding the values and norms that are non-negotiable for you. And by setting this framework you automatically make clear what leeway your employees have.

The SolutionCircle does not relieve the manager of the duty of responsible leadership. It serves as an effective instrument to achieve progress with the team in certain situations.

Appreciation and Tolerance When Hearing about Problems

The procedure described here requires care and recognition for situations that seem problematic. People perceive an event and experience it as uncomfortable or even as a threat. Any deviation from the desired state is described as a problem. Therefore, problems are described from the personal experience of the people concerned, and so it is sometimes hard for outsiders to understand them. Even when we cannot understand the problems other people tell us about, it must have been a difficult, sometimes even painful experience for them. When we brush off problems as unimportant or invalid, we are not doing justice to the emotional state of this person. This, by the way, is often the reason for resistance. Even if a problem seems banal or trivial to you at first sight, you should take it seriously. Moreover, for the employee it is not so easy to talk openly about problems in the team. This is not something you do every day and just this fact should be appreciated accordingly, for here you can see a first sign of an honest wish for change.

Giving Compliments

I am often touched when I discover unsuspected strengths in my conversation partner. Although it is not really part of typical working culture, I then dare to offer a compliment. Members of the team all have personal qualities and experiences that can be used in mastering difficulties. These qualities or resources – robustness in difficult times, the ability to work hard, a sense of humour, willingness to listen to others and to help, being able to draft precise project plans, being interested to learn more – these and others make up the strengths of the team members.

Compliments have to be meant seriously and should not be used as a manipulative communication trick. You should also not compliment when you only want to be friendly or nice. In such cases, the coach quickly loses credibility. Helpful compliments are founded on observation of real events communicated verbally or by actions.

In working with teams, compliments are surprisingly powerful. They support hope and confidence in the steps that need to be taken. In addition, they illuminate past strengths and successes that can be helpful for reaching the goals. You will probably remember this from your childhood: for a moment, think of a compliment that you were given in your childhood or youth. Often, these compliments affect our image of ourselves for the rest of our lives.

Serenity and Trust

Serenity can only develop when you are convinced that this conflict makes perfect sense and that it is a starting point for sensible development. This is very demanding, especially since it is almost impossible to determine beforehand what it is that makes sense in a given case.

Maybe you can also compare this to surfing. I am standing on the board, concentrating so that I can follow each movement of the waves easily, always with the wave and not against it. Beneath me, I can feel the incredible power of the water, roaring and raging. Every crest needs a trough. I have to recognise where the energies are – only then can I use them for my goal. But I can only do this when I am surfing the wave and not when I enter the maelstrom. From a balanced position of serenity and security, I can react with ease. SolutionSurfing – surfing on the solution wave – is easiest when I act with serenity and trust.

Various Choices

In difficult situations, teams often merely juxtapose solution A and solution B. They have to decide between these two positions – black or white. In the SolutionCircle, we do not think in black or white, and not even in all of the grey scales in between, we are thinking in the whole colour spectrum! Many colours find their place in the solution! In working with teams, we want to open up various options for action and fathom the room for manoeuvre. We ask for the third (and fourth and fifth) possible solution.

Keeping Neutral

Keeping neutral is another principle of the SolutionCircle. It is important that the person creating the framework for a solution does not take sides, especially in conflict situations. If everyone in the team, including the manager, is involved in a conflict, it seems sensible to call in an external coach to facilitate a workshop. Every team member should be confident that the coach facilitates the conflict resolution process without bias. If this is not the case, the whole work will end up as an alibi exercise.

Every contribution to the work is important and valuable – in our opinion there are no wrong contributions. The SolutionCircle is designed to enable the parties in a conflict to develop the resolution together. You as coach of the process welcome all ideas and contributions – the team decides which contribution can be used for reaching the goal (within the given framework, of course). If the coach takes sides, he or she produces resistance and endangers the implementation of the steps necessary for a solution!

SolutionSurfing

If you lead a team, you can probably tell a lot of stories about big and small turbulences that had to be mastered: differences of opinion between employees and their boss, unexpected problems, a clash of expectations with regard to the quality of the work, discontinued projects, customer complaints etc. These events are like waves – waves of the team dynamic, waves of change. There are at least three different ways of dealing with these waves:

- Resist the wave with all your power (I am the boss! I do not want any change!).
- Duck (maybe it is not so bad to be overrun, after all).
- Surf the wave (using the energy to reach the goal together).

You have to be fit, mentally and physically, courageous and enthusiastic to be able to use the power of the wave to move ahead. You have to look forward and not look back. Imagine standing on a perfect wave in the surf. You use the power of the wave to get to shore – you use a forward oriented power to get to your goal. You are highly concentrated, balanced, stand in the wave, hear the thundering under your board, and use the energy of the wave elegantly and with ease.

This is SolutionSurfing: you successfully use the team dynamic based on the four basic principles of the SolutionCircle.

SolutionSurfing stands for our way of dealing with challenges in the work place. SolutionSurfers have powerful attractive goals and concentrate on solutions and their successful implementation. They use the goal-oriented energy of the wave and don't get pulled under. SolutionSurfing establishes a balance in a world in which the obstacles are too often in the centre of our consciousness and activities.

Team turbulences are opportunities. Use the waves to get to the shore of your dreams. The four basic principles of the SolutionCircle can serve as your surfboard for an exciting ride to success.

4 The SolutionCircle Step by Step

'No problem can be solved by the same level of consciousness that created it.'

Albert Einstein

The eight steps described on the next pages can help you to solve complex situations in teams and achieve goals successfully as a team. The SolutionCircle is subdivided into eight steps for ease and clarity. Of course, every problem situation in a team is different from the next. Sometimes they arise unexpectedly in team meetings and need to be worked on immediately. In these situations you can use individual elements of the SolutionCircle directly – you can ask targeted questions to find out together what has already worked.

If the situation is very complex and tension is high, it is most efficient for the team to take a time-out and design and implement a special workshop on the specific issues together. Usually, a workshop of this kind is facilitated by one person – this can be the team manager or an external consultant. The eight elements of the SolutionCircle can provide a useful structure for the workshop.

The Hopscotch Principle

There is no set order for the individual elements of the SolutionCircle. It is more useful to adapt them to each given situation. Sometimes it makes sense to leave out two steps and come back to them later. The better you know the individual elements and the better you can use them, the easier it is to respond to the situation. Perhaps you can remember games like hopscotch that you played as a child, drawing the field onto the street with chalk, jumping around with other children. In hopscotch, you have eight squares with the numbers 1 to 8 – but you don't necessarily hop into them one after the other. You hop on one leg, two squares at a time, back, forward, with a half turn in mid-air – depending on where the stone lands. This way, you choose a suitable procedure for every situation. The four basic principles remain centrally important: focusing on a solution, working on the basis of what is already working, illuminating resources and changing perspectives. The individual elements in the SolutionCircle each reflect individual aspects of these basic principles.

Definition of Coach

In the following, I will use the term 'coach' for the person leading the team through the SolutionCircle: be it the project leader, the manager of a department, the internal human resources development manager or an external consultant. If you facilitate the SolutionCircle as coach, you will mainly ask solution-oriented question in order to create a framework for the process. The coach accompanies the group, orients him- or herself toward the agreed goals and works carefully and appreciatively.

His or her role is not to have his or her own way, suggest his or her own ideas, or give orders. For the process to be initiated and carried out successfully, the coach will have to give responsibility for the development of a sustainable solution to the team.

Overview of the Steps in the SolutionCircle

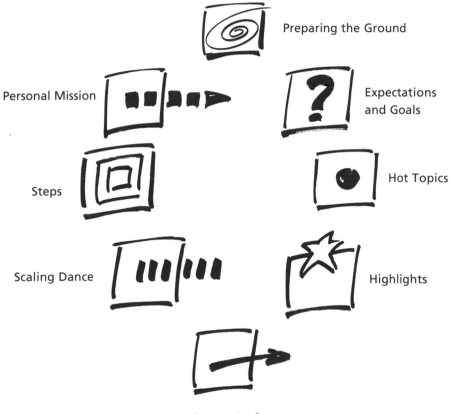

Preparing the Ground

Personal Mission

Expectations
and Goals

Hot Topics

Steps

Scaling Dance

Highlights

Future Perfect

Preparing the Ground

Goal

This first step serves to clarify the framework, to gain trust in the coach and agree on what is necessary for everybody to commit to collaborate enthusiastically.

The team members will usually enter into the process with very different assumptions about what is going to happen. Some may be a bit reluctant and insecure, others might be looking forward to being able to 'unload' at last. In this first step, it is most important to prepare to work together in the workshop so that everybody can join in without fear of being embarrassed or being treated unfairly.

Procedure
– Clarifying what brought us here

As coach, I first explain what brought us all to this room to work on this topic. I report to the group what happened in the conversations that led to this meeting, tell them about any agreements I have made and pass on any important information that I have been given. One very important point is clarifying the framework, including any non-negotiable factors.

– Naming resources that are already apparent to an outsider

As coach, you can tell the group what you have already heard about the team and try to list the special characteristics and successes of the team, stories and instances of high performance that make the team unique and that you find remarkable. You mention resources that you attribute to the team (even if you are an external consultant and have never worked with the team before). You can only do this with conviction – this is not about tactics. I only mention resources if I am personally convinced of them. So you can really only do this if you concentrated on this aspect in your preparation and consciously integrated it into your plans.

– An eye on the solution

At this point, it is useful to say something about working methods. In the workshop, it is less important to analyse the various problems thoroughly. Instead, we want to use most of the available time to develop solutions. The past is not the centre of attention, nor who made which mistake but rather the question of how we can co-create a successful, common future!

– Clarifying roles

It is important to make clear from the start the various roles. The coach's role is to create the framework and structure for the workshop, decide the process to be followed and ask questions, and the participants' role is to provide the content and develop the solutions.

– Establishing groundrules

You write down rules of conduct and communication that are important to the participants in order to enable an active participation. They can be labeled 'rules of collaboration' and agreed on as effective for this workshop.

It may be helpful to ask these questions:

- What rules of communication should we follow in this workshop so that everybody can participate comfortably?
- How will you know that we are discussing things factually

and not emotionally? What are we doing when we discuss this way? What are we not doing?

- Does everybody agree that we base our work today on these rules?

Example: Rules for the Workshop

- Whatever we discuss today will stay in this room (confidentiality).
- We will hear each other out.
- Everybody's opinion counts.
- The coach shall be impartial.
- Everybody can make a fool of himself in here.
- We will discuss facts and will stay calm.

Expectations and Goals

Goal

The goal of this step is to define the criteria for the success of the meeting. What goals have to be reached and what expectations have to be fulfilled to make participation worthwhile?

Here we define our common criteria against which we as team will eventually measure the success of our work. Sometimes these expectations are very diverse and also a bit unclear. In this step they are made more concrete and aligned. It is important to develop expectations and goals together and not to have them prescribed by someone else. This way the participants realise that we have an honest interest in everyone's needs and that committed participation by everybody is important and valuable. This helps increase their identification with the workshop and gives confidence that the outcome will have something to offer to every participant.

Procedure
Variation 1:

In smaller teams you can collect the expectations and goals on a flipchart. The coach can take time to ask everybody for their contribution. He or she can ask questions about the goal to find out exactly how things will look when these goals have been reached. These brief conversations are also interesting to the other team members and often help to clarify the issue and to increase understanding of each other.

Variation 2:

If you have a larger team (ten or more team members) you can also do this step in small groups.

a) Write down goals and expectations for this workshop in groups of three and four on a flipchart.

b) Display the flipcharts in the room.

c) Ask questions to clarify the statements and make individual statements more precise.

The different statements can be brought together on one flipchart and introduced quickly in the whole team using the team members' own words.

It may be helpful to ask these questions:

- What needs to happen in this workshop to make it really worth your time here?
- What should be different after the workshop?
- How will you know that you have reached this goal?
- If you reach this goal together, how will your customers notice?
- How probable is it in your view that your expectations of the workshop can be met?

Goals too high?

Normally teams are very realistic regarding their expectations. There are a few, however, that produce a huge list of expectations with very high goals. If you feel scepticism about the attainability of all of the goals, you can try to prioritise the list or ask about the probability of reaching the goals. It may be helpful to mention that the team is just starting a journey and they will get closer to their ambitious goals step by step.

Example: Expectations and Goals

Team member: This workshop will be successful if I finally get a chance to unload all the stuff that has been bothering me for a long time.

Coach: OK! So if we give you time and space to unload and say everything that is bothering you – what exactly will be different afterwards?

TM: I think that the other team members would realise then that they also make mistakes and would stop talking behind my back.

Coach: Let's say we actually manage to do this and the talking behind your back stops after today. Can you imagine this? (short pause.) The talking has stopped – what will you notice that it tells you it has stopped?

TM: (thinks) Hmm. I think I will notice that people look at me differently when I come back from the coffee break. They would be more open and direct. I would also get more open feedback. If I made a mistake, they would approach me directly and tell me what went wrong. Very direct feedback and not complicated in an e- mail or something.

Coach: If your colleagues did that, how would you react?

TM: I would probably also be more open and would maybe go to lunch with them more often. I imagine that I would probably also be more confident in what I do and would therefore make fewer mistakes. Additionally, I could be sure that I am doing a good job since if I am not getting any negative feedback, it would be OK.

Coach: Yes, that sounds very specific and tangible! What

	do you want me to put on the flipchart? How do you want to put your goal?
TM:	Hm. The goal is that the others stop talking behind my back!
Coach:	I like to put goals positively. What do you want the others to do instead?
TM:	For me the workshop will have been worthwhile if I can be sure that others criticise me directly in future.

Hot Topics

Goal

In this step, we determine the topics where improvement is aimed for.

Often, there are several overlapping topics. Sources of conflict are perceived with varying intensity by team members. In this step, we aim at making these diverse views apparent. Here, we can also set priorities: which topics should be tackled first?

Procedure

a) Every participant writes down on cards a few notes on less than optimal, or disturbing, or unsatisfactory experiences or situations. These cards are then displayed on the wall.

b) After everybody has pinned up their cards, the group is given the opportunity to clarify the meaning of individual cards. All the cards are left on the wall since they describe how someone experienced or perceived the situation. So justification or apologies are not necessary. If a discussion comes up, there should be room for it: exchanging different ways of perceiving the situation helps mutual understanding and clarifies the situation. However, one should try to keep this discussion as long as necessary and as short as possible.

c) The individual statements are clustered in groups and given headings. This can either be done with the team or you can take the lunch break and pre-sort the cards to present the suggested order to the group afterwards.

d) After the different headings have been formulated, a list of Hot

Topics is developed. This is especially necessary if many head-ings have been identified. Each team member can then decide which of the topics he or she finds really crucial and sign his or her name to it. This way, you get various groups of people that would like to work on particular topics. In this step it is less important to have the whole team work on one topic. It is good to let every team member contribute where he or she is willing to invest energy and commitment for change.

At the end of this step, you have several overall headings and groups of people who willing to work on the individual topics.

Comment

Some coaches leave out this phase. They see this third step as repeating the 'expectations and goals' phase – and moreover, they also find it very problem-oriented. The SolutionCircle can work without this step, too. Practical applications have shown that this phase is appreciated since it furthers the mutual under-standing in the team, especially in conflict situations. Often, individual team members can only look into the future after they had been given a suitable time to unload their negative experi-ences from the past.

Example: Hot Topics

In a team of sales people, the following list of hot topics emerged. The team had written down the exact words themselves – they were clear on what they mean. Here they are quoted to illustrate what these headings can look like:

- Unclear and conflicting sales structure
- Co-operation with others
- Leadership

- No knowledge transfer
- Dream team
- Team morale

Every one of these statements stands for a different experience of a team member, interpretations of other people's behaviour, perceptions and interpretations of statements and actions.

Out of the team of 10 people, two people ended up dealing with the topic 'dream team', five dealt with questions of 'sales structure' and three (including the manager) dealt with the topic 'leadership'.

Highlights

Goal

The participants start looking for situations in which the problem or the conflict either did not happen at all or was less severe. They find out which skills enabled them to accomplish this.

Things that worked in the past are often the first harbingers of practical solutions. Whereas the team had previously mostly focused on difficult situations, they now turn to all the occasions when something happened that the team liked so much that they want it to stay this way. Together with the team, we talk about highlights, start looking for successes and examine which resources made it possible for the team to achieve these successes.

To help the participants to take this step – which is not easy – it makes sense for the coach to give a short introduction, maybe like this:

> Now, probably not everything in this team is going wrong. If that were the case most of you would have already quit their jobs. So there must be highlights (successes) in the every day life of this team. Let's focus a moment on what is already working. After discussing what was difficult in the last month, let's now try to make the picture more rounded. Which highlights did you come across in the last weeks and months?

Procedure

If the team is small, the coach can collect highlights in the whole groups. He or she will ask questions of clarification, and acknowledge even small highlights appropriately, and thus reinforce resources.

In larger teams it is again more useful to work in small groups and then bring their highlights back into the plenary.

E-A-R-S

Highlights are exceptions, times when the difficulties did not occur, or occurred to a lesser extent. Therefore they offer an opportunity to explore situations when the participants showed resources that could also be used for a solution. The procedure that the coach follows, no matter how vague or cautious the team members are in describing what seem inconspicuous occurrences, can be summarised by the acronym: EARS (de Jong and Berg (1998)).

E: Eliciting the highlight, the exception. Often the participants mention small and unimportant highlights first. They are a bit vague and not really committed. If you don't listen well, it is easy to miss important exceptions where problems did not occur or occurred less.

A: Amplifying the exception, opening it up. You let the individual participants describe exactly how highlights are different from problem times. You explore how the exception became possible and especially the role the person telling about the exception played in it.

R: Reinforcing the successes, empowering. Acknowledging the highlights, taking time to explore them thoroughly, and giving compliments is a big part of the reinforcement.

S: Start again. The S reminds the coach to stay in this virtuous circle and go back again to ask 'and what else?'

It may be helpful to ask these questions:

- Which events in the last few weeks seem like a small highlight with regard to the issue at hand?
- What exactly was different?
- What did you contribute to enabling your colleague to react this way?
- If you say that you cannot find a highlight in the last months, maybe there was a situation in which the conflict was less severe? What did you contribute to that – what did others contribute?
- What can we learn from these highlights for the solution of the problem?

Example: Highlights

A company producing technical equipment employs many foreign workers whose tasks are mainly manual. In one of the production teams, the subject 'leadership' was mentioned as one of the 'hot topics'. Here are some quotes of the employees after they had looked for highlights regarding this topic in groups of three:

'We were backlogged. The team manager came to me to ask whether I would do overtime. I appreciated that he came to me to ask – you cannot simply assume that we will stay longer. When the team manager then thanked everybody personally later – that was really cool.'

'In project X, I was given total freedom to reach the goals agreed on. I could see that people really trusted me!'

'Most of the time they only talk to us if we make a mistake. When I suggested how we could improve our delivery process, the boss came over and praised me. That made me feel more secure and I felt better. I felt like he trusted me.'

'What I like about Ms M. was that she really listens very well and supports others when they have personal problems. She is the 'good soul' of this team and always makes time for everybody. She helped me once, when I was quarreling with another colleague.'

'I experienced one highlight, when the team manager asked me to help him show a new employee how we work here. This way, he got some help, and my work got a bit more exciting, because sometimes it gets a bit dull.'

Future Perfect

Goal

In the future perfect, the team designs a very precise picture of a future in which the problems have been solved.

The future perfect elegantly helps the team to construct future-oriented goals, making finding a solution much easier. This step focuses the attention on the level of solutions – and since we are talking of a 'perfect' future, everybody is allowed to describe a huge range of possibilities. The participants are encouraged to think broadly and to develop creative ideas.

Procedure

The future perfect is tackled by the interest groups that formed in the Hot Topics step. These groups are given the task of describing the ideal future of their topic as precisely as possible and writing it down. You can introduce this step this way, for example:

– For the next step, I would like to ask you a question that is a little bit strange. I am sure that it is very helpful for our purposes, but it needs a bit of imagination and creativity. Would you like me to ask this question?

Or like this:

– If we were very successful in this workshop and if the team could develop exactly as we want it to – where would the team be in two years time?

- What exactly would be different?
- What would the customers say about this team?
- If I meet the team again for some reason in two years time, what would I see, that told me something had changed for the better?

In the ensuing group presentations of the results of this step, it is important that every idea, every picture is seen as plausible and admissible. Saying 'this is not possible because ...' should be prevented. What we are aiming for here is simply exchanging visions and ideas.

After the group presentations, the coach can ask:

'Is this vision of the future attractive to the group that worked on it? Is there enough energy to start working in this direction?'

In smaller teams and if there is only one topic, the image of the future can also be worked on with the whole group.

Scaling Dance

Goal

The individual team members assess the current situation. We want to find out what has already worked well in the past.

Scales can be used in many different ways – they are a wonderful means of getting to the point. Scales are usually defined so that the highest number (normally 10) means the ideal state (the future perfect) and at the other end (at 1) you have the absolute opposite. Using scales also helps to get away from an either-or, black or white type of thinking. Many shades of grey are introduced, and the team can therefore be more discerning in their discussion.

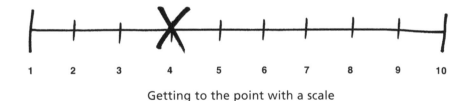

Getting to the point with a scale

When we use scales in the SolutionCircle, the difference between individual assessments of the team members (say one says 5, another says 9) are not relevant. What is interesting is why each assessment is as high as it is. We are curious about the difference between 1 and 5: what has already been achieved in getting to 5? Which resources were used?

The coach can draw the scales on a flipchart or mark them with tape on the floor. The participants then set markers or position themselves on a suitable place on the walking scale. When introducing this exercise, you have to be careful that the participants understand that the assessments are a momentary description of the situation and are therefore very personal and subjective. The personal assessments of different team members are not comparable since they are based on subjective perceptions. Scales are not very useful as a means of measuring average satisfaction but as a means of making the differences transparent and discovering the subtleties in the assessment.

Also in this step, the coach is free to ask individual team members for clarification. Larger groups can be asked to pair off to answer the question: 'What tells us that we have already reached X?'

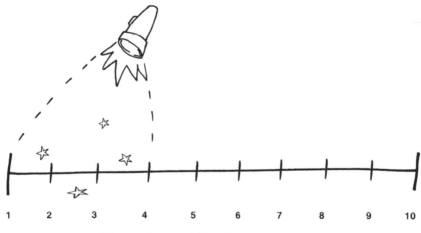

Discovering and illuminating resources

Principles for a Successful Scaling Dance
(Szabó (2005))

1. Introduction to Working with Scales
The Scaling Dance is a kind of reflection time for the team and is therefore different from the previous phase (developing future visions). Thus, it is important to have a clear transition to working with scales. Written scales on the flipchart or on the floor mark this new phase.

2. Trusting Perceptions and Assessments

Individual assessment of progress is surprisingly subjective. Using participants' very personal assessments as a basis for conversation has proven very useful. Instead of arguing about the differences between their own assessment and perception and their partner's, people should be encouraged to explore each other's evidence.

When introducing scaling questions, you should emphasise that individual assessments asked for are momentary and subjective and can always be changed again at a later time. There is no wrong assessment by the participants – every positioning is exactly right.

3. Don't calculate averages

Assessments on scales cannot be compared mathematically since they all are made according to subjective criteria. What a number 2 represents in the assessment of a team member can only be determined in conversation. Therefore, don't give in to the temptation to calculate a 'team average' out of the individual numbers.

4. Speaking about resources

Pose your scaling questions so that you get as much information about existing strengths and (hidden) skills as possible. Remember: talking about solutions creates solutions, talking about problems and deficits increases the problems. Progress is facilitated if you find out what you can already build on and which competences are available.

5. Using differences

The absolute value of the individual numbers is less important than the differences between the individual numbers. The differences between what we call a highlight and the current situation, differences between excellent examples and less excellent examples or differences between what you are not doing now but will do if you progress further, provide relevant information about possible solutions.

It may be helpful to ask these questions:

- Imagine a scale from 1 to 10. Where are you now with regard to the topic X where 10 stands for the ideal state (future perfect) and 1 stands for the exact opposite?
- How did you manage to get to this point? What is the difference between 1 and where you are now?
- If you think about your best highlight, where was it on the same scale. What is the difference here?
- What did you personally contribute to get you to X?
- How would you know that you have progressed just a small step towards 10?
- Which resources did you use to be able keep at X and not sink lower?

Example: Scaling Dance

A team of three managers in a small trust company hired an external coach to help them solve their conflicts.

Coach:	On a scale of 1 to 10, where 10 means that you can co-operate productively and successfully again, and 1 means that the conflict has become unbearable, where are you at the moment?
A:	Today, I am at a 6. Yesterday it was much lower, but today, yes, I think a 6 is correct.
Coach:	OK! How come that you are already that high?
A:	Our conversation today showed me that we actually agree on several crucial issues and that, in fact, we are pulling in the same direction. If only we could talk more in peace and quiet without the daily stress.

Coach:	And what else?
A:	(chuckles) At one point today, I was rather stubborn because the issue is very important to me. Sometimes I don't really think it's great that I'm that stubborn. However, today, for the first time in a long while, I felt that my stubbornness was accepted at least to a certain degree. I think that my being hardheaded also helped the conversation.
B:	Hmm. I am still at a 2.
Coach:	A 2. I guess, a lot needs to happen for you so that you can feel comfortable here in the team again – and yet, you are not at 0. What is it that is going well?
B:	Well? I don't really know exactly. The 2 rather expresses my hope that we can resolve our conflict.
Coach:	And what gives you this hope?
B:	For the first time, today, I understood what my partners really meant. We listened to each other.
Coach:	Where on the scale, do you think you will be working well again?
B:	Hmm. I think that we'll start being productive at a 4.5.
Coach:	OK! Can you imagine what you could do to get just a very small step closer to 4.5?
B:	When we started our business, at the beginning of our time together, when we were still travelling to customers together, we still had time for one another while travelling: there was no agenda. Today, I realise that I miss this time for swapping ideas. I

would like to reintroduce some form of regular exchange.

C: Yes, I think this is a good idea – and it raises my assessment a little bit. I am now on a 2.5.

Steps

Goal

In this step we design concrete measures that the team can implement in the near future – the sooner the better.

It is easy to find steps on the basis of the Scaling Dance. You simply note what needs to be done to get a small step closer to 10.

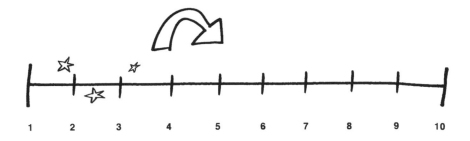

Taking a small step forward

Support during the Implementation Phase

In this step, you also note people the team could turn to for support as an additional help for the implementation phase. For example, you can ask other outsiders like colleagues from other departments, superiors or even customers. Supporters can be helpful in different ways. Sometimes it is enough to tell somebody outside the team what changes are planned. You gain more commitment and maybe also new ideas.

Keeping the Process Going

It is important that the team is clear about how they can keep the process going. What agreements do they need to keep working on the solutions they have talked about? How are they going to talk about progress? If members of the team want to change themselves (and it is essential that this is voluntary), positive reinforcement and feedback is called for. If their first attempts at doing something different go unnoticed, they are soon discontinued. Keeping the process going means asking what has improved and also immediately focusing on useful behaviour. This can happen in various ways, and teams most often have very productive ideas themselves.

It may be helpful to ask these questions:

- What do you need to get one step closer to 10?
- What can you contribute to move things forward a bit?
- How would you notice that the situation has changed just a little bit for the better?
- If this scale could talk, what would it recommend as your next step?
- What would your customers say if you implement this measure? How would your customers notice the difference?
- How are you going to exchange and note the first small successes in the implementation?

Example: Steps

Every two weeks, there is a meeting of the eight head nurses who each lead a ward in a provincial hospital. Their aim is to improve their meeting culture and thereby become more efficient. They would be one step higher on the scale, when

- the meeting starts punctually;
- more notice is given for the meeting;
- standard procedures are decided on by two nurses before-hand and introduced for information only, not discussed in the meeting;
- they decide beforehand how much time they are going to use for each item on the agenda (manage this flexibly);
- they also take votes instead of having endless discussions.

One of the head nurses commented that she would know that they are one point closer to 10 when:

- the meeting ends before nine thirty pm;
- I feel like going to the cafeteria together after the meeting;
- I get the feeling that the others are interested in my department: they ask me questions and give suggestions;
- I don't think about other things while the others are talking.

Personal Mission

Goal

By giving an observation task or an action-oriented task, attention is directed to certain aspects of the implementation which continue supporting the process in the team's day-to-day life.

A personal mission or task is an elegant way of continuing to support the process in the daily work life of the team and to keep the participants focused on success. By focusing attention on small and large successes the process is accelerated constructively.

This step can be stated as an observation task: the individual team members focus explicitly on changes in the desired direction over the next couple of days and write them down. In a team meeting or in a further small workshop, these observations are exchanged.

Alternatively, the personal task can involve action: every team member is to think of a concrete measure that they themselves find suitable to support the team process constructively. This personal measure is to be implemented in the near future – without telling anybody about it.

A personal task once again integrates all participants of the workshop in a process of development. Everybody can invest as much as he or she deems sensible – but everybody has to invest something.

Example: Personal Mission

At the end of a three day workshop with the three managers of a social services company, the central question was how to develop a more sustainable lifestyle. Everybody was investing so much energy and time into their jobs that their work-life balance was unhealthy. The internal coach in the human resources department gave each of them the following personal task:

> Do not change anything at the moment. However, at home, place a bowl in a nice spot and next to it, put a whole bag of your favourite sweets. Every evening, when you come home, think about how well you treated yourself today. If you feel drained and unsatisfied – put one sweet into the bowl. If you are mostly satisfied with yourself – two sweets. If you think: 'This is exactly how I would like things to be in the future', you put three sweets into the bowl. After one week, you can see what happened.

He got this mail from one of the managers after two days:

> ... I have already put out a bowl and sweets. What is more impressive, however, is that the image of the bowl and the thought that there is going to be a critical review of the day stays with me all day. Especially when I have to decide what to do, this image is present and reminds me 'just in time' at crucial moments to think carefully about my priorities. The image of the bowl has already fulfilled the purpose of the exercise. THANKS again for this idea.

5 Setting Up a Workshop with the SolutionCircle

'If you don't have a grip on everything, at least you have your hands free!'

Leading or accompanying a team – especially in problem or crisis situations – is a personal adventure. You need courage to confront situations where the process cannot be planned. Team dynamics are uncertain; personal learning comes from the exciting changes happening in the team.

Preparation and Planning are Reassuring

If you have ever gone on a hiking trip in the mountains for several days, you know how important preparation and planning are. You have to buy maps and get information on the route. You may need new hiking boots. The backpack has to be packed well, so that you have everything that is necessary but not too much, so that you can still carry it.

You have to organise a place to sleep. Perhaps you should also work on your stamina beforehand. Preparation and planning provide safety – but they do not guarantee success. What if the weather changes and you suddenly face a storm? What if you inadvertently pull a muscle on the way? What if the marked hiking path has been swept away in a storm or the owner of the alpine hut did not buy enough supplies, and you and your co-hikers do not get a packed lunch for the second day?

The best planning and preparation may not help – in such situations you are called upon personally. You have to be able to adjust to the new situation flexibly and intuitively.

Planning rates highly in organisations. If you plan, you are deemed future oriented, risk aware, and goal focused. However, plans cannot predict the future, nor do they necessarily lead to the desired outcome in complex systems. To give an example, only one week after the invasion of Iraq, the generals had to admit: 'The enemy that we are fighting against is a different enemy than the one that we fought against in our simulations.' Just a few days were enough for reality to catch up with the planning.

Planning in the Face of Uncertainty

In organisations, projects are thought through as carefully and as competently as possible – and still we often see projects that have come to a stop because people do not know how to proceed, unforeseen things have happened or people reacted very differently from what was expected.

It is very similar with the SolutionCircle method described here: I prepare myself carefully in the planning phase. As a team manager, I have an image of the team based on my experience and knowledge of the team – and then I find a totally different situation. I have worked with teams that changed their goals during the workshop, questioned them again, redefined them. Or working groups that had solemnly declared how much they wanted a change before the workshop and then during the workshop rejected even the smallest innovation. And of course, I have met team members that reacted very differently in the workshop from what I had expected.

Planning itself involves a certain risk – the image of the world that I construct for myself can turn into blinkers. You need flexibility to amend your image, to adjust quickly and react according to the situation. You need composure and calmness to let your planning go and courage to go into a situation that you did not expect.

In this book, you will find tools that you can pack into your backpack before you start on your adventure. The SolutionCircle as a method can serve as your map, on which a possible route is marked. However, **you** are central. It is not so much the detailed knowledge of the tools or the meticulous utilisation of the procedure that guarantee the success of the SolutionCircle. It is the creativity and delight in customising the various tools to make them fit the different situations you encounter. Don't stick stubbornly to your plans, but instead find a kind of experimental way of dealing with uncertainty. Sometimes you can be rather intuitive. Sometimes you are a sort of researcher who introduces the next step responsibly and experimentally and observes what happens. Find out what works and what fits. Build on your intuition since if you want to master the adventure team successfully, you yourself provide the crucial factors: your experience, your flexibility and your appreciative attitude.

Appreciation and Responsibility
When we are talking about and dealing with uncertainty in an experimental way, we always combine this playful approach with responsibility and appreciation. The most important thing is to observe and listen attentively and then ask the next question or introduce the next step on the basis of what you heard or observed. It is not about mechanically reproducing prefabricated steps but about entering a circle. Observe the reactions to your interventions carefully. Focus on what happens, and then decide on your next intervention. This process is decisive for reaching the goal and developing a suitable solution.

Checklist for Personal Preparation

The following questions help the team manager to prepare for the workshop:

- Am I a suitable person to facilitate the workshop (personal involvement, independence, willingness to hold back my own ideas and plans and let the team take the responsibility for developing a solution)?

Personal Goals

- What do I want to achieve with this workshop?
- What else?
- How will I know that the workshop has been successful?

Clarifying the Goal of the Workshop

- What exactly is the goal of the workshop?
- When we have worked on our topics successfully, what will be different after the workshop? What will my team members do differently?
- What will I gain, what will the team gain, when we reach our goals?
- What could be a motto or a title for the workshop?

My Job as Coach/Facilitator

- If I as coach/facilitator did a really good job in the workshop, what would the team members say then?
- How would I know I had done a good job?
- What else could be helpful in facilitating the workshop?

Realising the Resources of the Team

- What have we as team already mastered successfully (in the areas of performance, learning and enjoyment)?

- What two resources do I especially appreciate in my team?
- What would others (customers, other departments, superiors) say are the strengths of our team?
- What have we already tried in looking for a solution?

Clarifying the Framework

- What cannot be changed: by the company, by the market or by me as a leader?

Crucial Success Factors

When working with the SolutionCircle, you have certain minimal prerequisites without which an intervention makes little sense.

There is a simple formula by the Chilean coach Julio Olalla that shows what is necessary, if you want to implement changes successfully.

Will

✗

Times

Appeal of the goal

✗

Times

Confidence in its feasibility

✗

Times

Clarity of the first concrete step

Must be greater than

The effort involved

SolutionCircle's sphere of influence

The four factors described here are crucial for the success of the implementation of change processes. They are connected by the mathematical principle of multiplication, making their interdependence obvious. The result stays 0 as long as one of the factors is 0: if I do not want to tackle an issue, nothing will happen. If I tackle the issue but do not have the least inkling of what is in it for me, I will hardly get started. If I want to do something and I have a clear goal but don't believe that what I want is feasible, it would be stupid even to start. And if the will, the goal, and belief in the feasibility are all there, but I don't know what my first step could be, I will not be able to take that first step either.

The SolutionCircle makes it possible to influence the last three factors (appeal of the goal, confidence in the feasibility, and clarity of the first step) to a certain extent. The factor 'will' however cannot be influenced from the outside.

A Minimal Willingness to Change

There has to be a minimal consensus in the team that the situation as they perceive it at the moment needs to change. If there is no problem, if nobody is interested in developing team work, even the best method will not be useful. This willingness to change can hardly be influenced from outside.

Clarifying the Responsibility for the Change

Additionally, it is important to state clearly from the beginning that it is not the coach who is responsible for a successful result but the participants. Teams in difficult situations tend to hand over their responsibility – if you as team manager then accept it, you create an intensive dependency. Success may seem obvious at first (conflict solved!), but in the background and in the long run, the problems will continue to smoulder and break out again at the first opportunity.

With the SolutionCircle and its associated tools, you provide a framework in which working on a solution becomes possible. You are responsible for the process and thereby support the team in finding their solution.

Your Interest as Manager

Not every conversation can be organised in the form of a SolutionCircle – sometimes as manager you have clear interests, have to communicate certain facts, have to set goals or pass on complaints that have come to you in your role as manager of the team. Here it would be pointless to hold back since in these situations, clarification of your leadership principles or of the framework is called for. In this case, you cannot resort to the role of a neutral facilitator, but you have to take a position – and that can be done appreciatively, too.

Typical Agenda for a One-Day Team Workshop

Twelve managers of a small company met for a retreat workshop on the topic 'increasing effective collaboration'. What was most important was the optimisation of their internal processes and increasing the efficiency of their meetings. The retreat was led and facilitated by the human resource manager. This is his agenda for the day:

Time	Topic	Activity	Remarks
08:30am	**Clarifying framework**	Clarifying the background to this retreat. Introduction to the topic. What resources do we have? Every participant reports identified strengths and skills of every other participant.	Human Resource Manager

08:40am	'Domestic' details	Time, breaks, procedure	
08:50am	**Goals and Expectations**	Collecting goals on the flipchart.	Collect on flipchart
		What needs to happen today, to make it useful...	Check for understanding,
		Finding overall headings for the goal.	
09:20am	**Scaling Dance**	Where am I at the moment regarding my/our goals?	Mark scale on the floor
		Is this a good place? Where would I have to stand to be content? Where could I realistically get to today?	
		In groups of four: What exactly put me at X? So what is already working well? What resources can be deduced from this?	Group discussion Write down results on flipcharts
10:00am	**Break**		
10:15am	**Scaling Dance**	Plenary presentation	Questions, reinforcing, differentiation.
11:15am	**Short Input**	'How change succeeds' Short input according to the model of J. Olalla	(If appropriate here)
		Will to tackle an issue **x** **appeal** of the goal **x** **confidence** in the feasibility **x** **clarity** of the concrete steps must be larger than the **effort for the change**	

11:45am	**Light Lunch**		
1:30pm	**Future Perfect**	If this succeeds: – What will be different? – What will I do differently? – How will the people in around me notice? What are they going to say?	Individual work
1.45pm	**Future Perfect**	Exchanging results, collecting them on flipchart	Groups of four (weather permitting solution walk)
2:25pm	**Future Perfect**	Plenary presentation. Prioritising: which are the most attractive ideas?	Questions, Surprise, Astonishment
3:30pm	**Break**		
3:45pm	**Measures**	Collecting ideas that could take the team a small step towards the future perfect.	Collect on flipchart. Questions What exactly is everybody doing? How will the others know?
4:15pm	**Check**	Are we on track? What else would be important now? What about our goals? What else would be helpful now?	
4:30pm	**Keeping the process going**	Introducing regular scaling in the meetings 10 minutes before the end.	Show with the example of confidence scale (how confident for change)

4:45pm	**Next steps**	Defining together: next meeting, communication of results . . .	
	Observation **Experiment**		What did I notice?
5.15 pm	**End**		

6 Dealing with Strong Personalities

'We all have a world inside, each his or her own. But how are we to understand ... if I put the meaning of things into my words as I perceive them whereas the listener inadvertently interprets them with the meaning of things that belong to his world.'

Luigi Pirandello

The World is Created in your Head

In your team, opinions are exchanged, people have arguments and employees may have opinions different from yours – you think they are inappropriate or wrong. But are you sure that you are right?

Different opinions are often connected to the way reality is perceived – and perception is very subjective. If you ask three people who witnessed an accident in the street, every one of them will give you a different account. A statement by a department manager may cause one team member to be offended, whereas a second team member does not think twice about it. We create our image of the world based on our opinions, our expectations and our convictions. Paul Watzlawick, the communication scientist and constructivist, wrote a wonderful story about this in his book 'The

Situation Is Hopeless, But Not Serious: The Pursuit of Unhappiness' (W. W. Norton & Company, 1983).

> *A man wants to hang up a picture. He has the nail, but no hammer. His neighbour has one. And so our man decides to go next door and borrow it. But he hesitates: 'What if my neighbour won't lend me the hammer? Yesterday he was in such a hurry when he greeted me so hastily. Perhaps he was in a hurry. But perhaps the haste was only an excuse: maybe he has something against me? Well, what? I haven't done anything to him: it's just his imagination. If someone wanted to borrow a tool from me, I would give it to him right away. Then why won't he? People like this idiot are the ruination of others. And he also thinks I'm dependent on him for his hammer, just because he has a hammer. I've had it up to here'. And so he storms to his neighbour's house and rings the bell. The neighbour opens the door, but before he can say his friendly 'Good morning' our man shouts at him 'You can just keep your hammer, you idiot!'.*

Even if this story seems hopelessly exaggerated, it corresponds closely to our way of acting in the world. The man achieved something astonishing: within a short time, he convinced himself that his neighbour was an unfriendly and really disagreeable person and really not to be trusted him. Whether this is true or not – our man is convinced. For him, this is the truth!

This means that a problem for one person is not necessarily a problem for somebody else. Everyone perceives some situations as problematic, does not feel accepted, interprets statements in a certain way, has hypotheses about what the other person could have meant. Problems arise from individual perception and are really only constructs, only seen as real, as independent of the moment and the particular situation by the person affected. On this basis, the judgment 'true' or 'false' that we are prone to reach all too quickly in every day life is void. The question is: 'What is appropriate?' My personal experiences, my knowledge, and my personality lead me to interpret statements in my own way. Nobody goes out of his way to perceive something as 'wrong' – but maybe his perception or interpretation does not match what the other person wanted to say. Usually, these personal interpretations cause feelings which lead him to do or say something in response. This process is absolutely individual. This is what makes communication between human beings so fascinating, exciting, and so prone to disruption. If we look at the patterns of communication and perception described above, it is actually a very lucky coincidence that two people understand one another at all.

In his book 'Erfolgreich führen und leiten' (Successful Leadership), Jürgen Hargens uses the example of a permeable wall. Imagine you think that a wall is soft and permeable. This is how you see this wall in your thoughts. Your attempt to prove your theory will at best result in a big bump on your head.

So what do you know in an absolute sense? You can be relatively sure that your interpretation does not fit. The wall that you tested for permeability proved to be hard and solid – what the wall is really made of, you still don't know. So you will venture to create a new interpretation that you hope fits better.

It might also be that you test your hypothesis 'a wall is permeable' in Japan. There a few walls – those made of paper – are actually permeable and your interpretation would suddenly fit.

In your team, you will always meet members with different opinions from yours. There are members who label the wall permeable, semi-permeable or not permeable at all, members that choose another interpretation of the world. In the SolutionCircle, we do not concentrate on finding out whose is 'correct' or 'false' but we try to find out how the different opinions can be made useful for reaching the joint goal. The central concern is to enter into a conversation with people who advocate a different opinion and to talk about what could be useful and sensible in reaching the goal.

In this context, being useful in reaching the goal means finding out how other opinions can contribute to make the goal more concrete and to widen it, as well as to show what could help to start concrete steps in the desired direction. Working with the SolutionCircle, you are always oriented toward the goal which can be labeled very differently: profit, revenue, job-satisfaction, performance, full employment, learning etc. Without defining all these labels together, it is difficult to ascertain progress in the direction of the goal. If you are dealing with companies, parts of the goal are usually pre-determined and non-negotiable – every company wants to survive in the market. If this is not the goal of the team or the individual team members, they are simply in the wrong place.

Different opinions should be met with appreciation since the ideas and perceptions of others can help to differentiate the goals and make them more precise. This way it becomes easier to determine procedures that are truly tailored to the team.

Practising Tolerance

The biggest challenge in working with the SolutionCircle is staying in a constructive conversation with people with different opinions! Maintaining and practising your tolerance of other opinions and ways of seeing the world is of utmost importance. This is the only way in which you can discuss your differences productively and discuss how they can contribute to reaching the goals together.

It is often hard work not to label other opinions as wrong or incorrect but instead to think about their possible contribution, their meaning and the opportunities they offer. It will help your partner in conversation to feel taken seriously – simply because you are interested in his or her ideas. Dealing with other points of view also helps you learn for yourself and develop new ideas.

Staying in Conversation with Strong Personalities

People advocating divergent opinions are often strong personalities. Sometimes, they are people who eloquently and imperturbably defend their point of view. Sometimes they are stubborn or don't really want to change – and in all of that they are hardheaded. Or in other words, they

- are persevering.
- are willing to question existing positions.
- know where they stand and don't change their opinions lightly.
- are willing to take risks.

Even though we are working with teams, we should not forget that teams are made up of individual personalities. In order to develop the team as a whole, it is helpful in many situations to turn to the individual and pose questions oriented at developing a solution directly with him. Ask direct questions, have short conversations in front of everybody else – stay in conversation with the respective individuals. Don't be afraid that this could be boring for the others. Normally, the opposite is true.

Suggestions for Typical Situations

When you start working with the SolutionCircle, you will soon discover that there are situations that regularly come up in this or a similar form. Apart from team members of a totally different opinion, you will also meet those that have no opinion at all. Knowing some of these starting points can be helpful for gaining professional skills in dealing with them.

Strong Personalities 'just visiting'

You often meet people in the team who don't really know why they are in the workshop – in fact, it is everybody else who needs to change: be it the boss, the human resource developer, the whole board of executives. Personalities of the type 'everybody else should ...' are characterised by their belief that it is not in their power – or not their job – to solve the current problem.

If somebody in the team behaves in this way, you need a lot of patience. Normally, these people cannot subscribe to a goal and even less design one themselves. For these visitors, there is nothing that warrants any effort at the moment.

Three ways of dealing with 'visitors' have been helpful:

a) Demonstrating patience and trusting that this person will be 'infected' by the team dynamic or will find their own access to the solution.

b) Complimenting them in a way that shows understanding for their position. For example:

> Max, I am very impressed that you have come here today even though you don't really see the sense of this workshop. It would obviously have been possible for you to take the simple route and stay away ... I guess, it is not easy for you to be here and spend valuable time talking about things that you really do not want to talk about. I also realise that you have your own opinion on a lot of things. I hope you can continue to use this strength for the team. This could be a very valuable contribution for everyone.

c) We cannot change people at the push of a button. Often questions that target the interdependencies between individual behaviours are useful:

'If the top management did what you want, what effect would that have on you? What would you be doing differently then?'

'Is there any way of helping the top management behave in this way?'

'Suppose the top management do not change their behaviour in the future. Would you be interested in finding out how you could manage to deal with the others better so that you can work more efficiently in the future?'

Strong Personalities as Complainants

People are used to talking about their worries. When a workshop to work on conflicts has been scheduled, everybody really hopes that a solution to the problem will be presented to them – or at least that they get a chance to complain at length. If you try to actively steer the conversation towards the solution, often a new problem crops up; the team again descends into the depths of complaint and moaning.

Complainants are people who don't seem to really want to achieve a solution to the problems. They often feel powerless with regard to the problem and don't really see a chance to change something themselves. Often they do not even know what they want to change and seem to be saying: 'It's not going to work anyway!'

In this context, when you are working with the SolutionCircle, asking solution-building questions is almost certain to lead people onto the level of solutions. So actually, what you do is you go into the basement with them and provide them with a staircase that leads back to the level of solutions.

If you have a whole team in front of you that has a culture of complaining, a short reminder that we really want to use the time effectively is often helpful:

> 'I can see that some of you have a hard time behind you. I am really impressed that you have managed to keep up such a high level of quality in your work. Now we have come together to talk about solutions. What do you think, do you want to venture out and try to define goals and develop concrete solutions in the remaining time?'

Strong Personalities in Resistance

Every so often you meet team members who seem to to you to be 'resistant': they are against change, want the procedures to be different, reject suggestions of other team members or shake their heads in silence.

As in the other cases above, it helps to talk directly to the person to find out what motivates him to work with the group in this way:

> 'Are we still on track with regard to the goal? What could we do in your opinion to get closer to the goal?'

> 'What exactly do you need now? – What would the solution have to look like for you? – What other elements are important to you?'

Strong Personalities as 'Know-It-Alls'

Their behaviour is characterised by their belief that they actually know the solution as well as the goal and their only expectation of the workshop that everybody else will accept their solution. They know – thanks to their long years of experience in the company – how things work. They know how things should really be and don't miss a chance to stress this.

As coach, you can take up their suggestions and appreciate them, acknowledging that their extensive experience is important to the team. You stress that the team has choices and that everybody is looking for a customised, suitable solution for the whole team. The suggestions of the 'know-it-all' can be tested along with everybody else's. In this case, try to stay engaged and leave enough room for everybody else to develop further ideas and suggestions for solutions.

Two Scenes from a Workshop

As an example, here are two scenes from a workshop led by the department manager. Two months previously, two new employees had joined the department. Since then, the atmosphere in the team had deteriorated remarkably. Processes were not working as smoothly as they used to. In a department meeting, the team decided to deal with these problems together.

Scene 1: Expectations for the workshop

Manager:	'Margaret, what should be different after the workshop in your opinion?'
Margaret:	'I don't know. Everybody thought we should have a meeting so that we can to work together better again. So this is why I am here, too. I appreciate what the others said.'
Manager:	'OK! So what needs to happen in the next two hours so that you can be content and won't feel that you have wasted your time?'
Margaret:	'... Well, I am simply here because everybody else thought that we should have this meeting. I am new here, and I don't even know how it was before I came. I just hope that we don't need two hours because I still have a lot to do. Actually, I really don't know what should happen here.'
Manager:	'I really appreciate your openness. I feel that you are willing to join in even though you are not quite clear on

the point of all of this, and you don't know where this is going. I see that you are very loyal to the team. Thank you. I guess that this is not very easy for you. If in the course of the workshop you have an idea of what could be important for you, please don't hesitate to say so.'

Scene 2: An hour or so later

Felix:	'I think this discussion is pretty tiring. We aren't going anywhere, nothing is happening. This way, it is going to take ages and we won't end up with concrete results to take back. Before, we never had to discuss these topics. Things ran smoothly, and everybody simply knew what needed to be done!'
Tom:	'Felix is right. Couldn't we just get to the point, and instead of going round in circles, speed up a bit? Our job descriptions state exactly what everybody has to do. You just have to do it.'
Manager:	'Sure, Felix. I can see that you are getting impatient.'
Felix:	'No, I am not getting impatient. I simply want to move on and stop being deadlocked!'
Manager:	'How useful or how efficient was what we have done so far for you – on a scale of 1 to 10?'
Felix:	'A two at most.'
Manager:	'OK! And where on the scale would we have to get to in the end?'
Felix:	'To an 8.5!'
Manager:	'So far, what has been so useful in our conversation that you put it at a 2?'
Felix:	'Margaret and Sue told us a bit about their previous jobs. That was new and good. Also asking about what is already working after two months – I think that moved us forward a bit.'

Manager:	'Yes, I also thought that was helpful. Do you have an idea of how we could raise your assessment by one or two points during the next half hour?'
Felix:	' ... We are constantly talking about flexibility in dealing with our customers. I would like to know what exactly everybody means by "flexibility". What does it look like when we are being flexible? And – what would be good, would be if we had a flowchart of our central operating procedures. We could start work on it later on: collect step by step who has to do what and where the interfaces are.'
Tom:	'Yes, the suggestion about the flowchart would be helpful. Then we would have it in black and white on paper.'
Manager:	'Does everybody else agree that we take the topic "flexibility" and then turn to the operating procedures? I would like to wind up the topic that we were just discussing first. I have two more questions concerning that topic, and it won't take longer than 10 minutes. Is that OK?'

7 A Look in the Toolbox

'It is better to know some of the questions than all of the answers.'

James Thurber

Solution Finding Questions

Asking questions is – as we have already mentioned several times – the most important tool in the SolutionCircle. By asking questions we direct our thinking to the development of a solution. Proceeding with curiosity, as if carrying out a research project, is the best way of making fascinating discoveries. As a side effect, this means that we will be constantly expanding our knowledge. Often we don't even realise that we are learning.

Solution finding questions can be divided into different categories. Now, which question best fits the situation at hand? There is a very simple rule of thumb: the longer it takes for someone to answer the question the more confident you can be that you asked an effective question. Don't disturb your partner's thought process by reformulating the question or asking again. Have the patience to wait until your partner has found and formulated an answer.

Fear that the question is not appropriate or will be misunderstood is usually groundless. If a question is perceived as unsuitable or not clear, clients normally say so quite quickly. So practise being patient, and don't interrupt the important process of finding an answer. This is the time when new insights emerge. Experienced coaches say that they count to two hundred very slowly in this 'sacred time'. Should the client not have found the answer by then, simply start counting from the beginning . . .

Nevertheless, there are many different ways of asking questions. Some questions are used to achieve one's own goals. You probably know situations where questions are used to intimidate someone and make it more difficult to respond. The questions in the SolutionCircle are not an end in themselves. They are there to serve a purpose: to help define the goal more clearly, to optimise resources and to design concrete steps for implementation.

Solution finding questions are characterised by their clarity and simplicity. In the following, we have structured the questions into six different types to help you enlarge your repertoire of questions and find a selection of effective questions for every situation.

Type 1: Asking for the Goal

When you are working with your team, you won't be very interested in 'off-the-shelf' goals, but you will want goals that are motivating and customised to your particular situation. You steer towards focusing your energies and achieving what you strive for together. Formulating common goals means creating a future that you want to belong to.

It has proven very useful to invest enough time for the definition of the goal. The more you talk about it, the clearer and more important it becomes. It is important to be very concrete when it comes to future behaviour. The goal 'better communication' is a bit vague and unclear. What exactly is different when you are communicating better as a team? How will the team members behave when they have reached their goals? How are others going to notice it? What will be the effects of the team reaching its goal?

Goals are well defined when they are specific and refer to concrete behaviour.

Characteristics of clearly defined goals:

* The goal should be defined with reference to its content, scope, and time period:
  'After this workshop I want to have two measures that we can implement in the next few weeks in order to improve our internal communication!'
* Implementation of the goal should be fully within the team's control.
* Small goals are better than ones that are too large.
* The goal should be expressed as the beginning of something (rather than the end of something). 'Toward the goal' and not 'away from the problem.' When you hear: *'My boss should stop criticising me all the time'*, ask *'What should he do instead?'*
* The description of the goal should describe the behaviour of the client/team member and the reactions of others (interactional).
  'Suppose you act this way in the future, how do you think the marketing department would react to this changed behaviour?'
* It should be something that seems like 'a miracle', or at least it should go in that direction. Attractive goals are inspirational.
* The goal should be concrete and behavioural. *'What exactly will you be doing differently when you have reached your goal?'*
* The goal should take into account non-negotiable elements of the situation.

(Source: Steve de Shazer)

If you succeed in drawing a landscape that is attractive and motivational by asking goal oriented questions, you have mastered a central step: the desire for change becomes tangible.

These kinds of questions are often a bit hypothetical. They ask the team to be willing to 'beam' into the future with their thoughts. You act out this future scenario together, and you test possible variants: potential effects of future actions and behaviours are explored. In this way we support the option of deciding for or against an action or behaviour.

Useful Questions

- What exactly are you aiming for?
- When you have reached your goal, what exactly will be different?
- What will let you know that you have reached your goal? What will you notice?
- Suppose you reach your goal, how would the others in the team react?
- Suppose you reach your goal, what other effects would that have?
- Can you visualise your goal? Where are you in that picture and where are the other people concerned?
- Suppose the conflict at hand is resolved; what issue should your boss tackle next?
- Suppose your team chooses your way of proceeding in this project. How would your customers react?

Type 2: Questions about the Route to a Solution

How will the team get from where it is today to the desired landscape of the goal? With questions about the route to the solution you can develop ways of getting from the problematic situation now, towards the goal landscape. Perceivable actions and behaviour are again at the centre of attention. We ask about what every person is doing concretely and what the effects of these actions are.

In the SolutionCircle, we aim at asking about our actions in the 'here and now' and about developing alternative ways of acting in the future. By doing so we introduce the possibility of shaping the future. Finding out how you can come closer to your goal is a very exciting and thrilling process since often it is not one particular action that will take us a step further, but in our conversation we create various opportunities and alternatives that open up completely new choices.

Useful Questions

- What can you do starting tomorrow morning to take a step towards the goal?
- How can you support others in taking a step towards the goal?
- Who can you ask to support you in reaching your goal?
- Which personal resources could help you to reach your goal?
- Which behaviour of yours has already worked a bit toward a solution?
- What would experts (or a good friend of yours) advise you to do next in this situation?
- How would other people notice that you have made a step towards the goal?
- How would you know that you have come a step further?

Type 3: Questions about Resources

It is common for teams to come across turbulent situations. These can be conflicts, problems or change processes that have been initiated too quickly and need to be mastered successfully. To do this the team faces the challenge of finding energy, personal skills and competencies again and again. Re-establishing the ability to work productively and to be successful is easier if the team is conscious of its strengths and able to utilise these strengths at will. Questions about existing resources can help to accomplish this. Often, we have to discover them anew.

Questions about resources make the skills of the individual and the skills of the whole team transparent. They help to find existing conscious and unconscious strengths that support the team to master the process successfully together. Often team members are surprised at the skills they discover in themselves and in others – and often the coach is surprised, too. Once you have discovered the resources, it is important to reinforce them because these resources are the basis for a sustainable solution.

Asking for highlights is helpful for discovering resources: exceptional situations in which the problems were perceived as less acute, less difficult or less stifling make it easier to realise what exactly is the difference between 'really bad' and 'bearable'. Usually, these are small signs of behaviour that is only slightly different. By doing this, we also show that these situations are not flukes, but that each of us has the ability to influence every situation personally. Highlights are in this sense 'harbingers of the solution' since they give concrete hints about what an attractive future could look like.

Useful Questions

- When during the last few weeks did this conflict/problem not occur, or when was it less intense?
- Can you describe those occasions in detail: what exactly was different?
- What did you do on those occasions to make the situation different?

- What would one of the people concerned say was different and what would they say you did differently?
- How have you managed to cope with this difficult situation so far?
- What attempts at a solution have you already tried?
- What gives you the confidence that a change for the better is possible at all?
- If there was something you did right in this difficult situation – what would that be?

Type 4: Scaling Questions

Working with scales is very effective to add dimension to a question. Especially in topics like communication, flexibility, customer orientation or leadership, scaling questions are very effective in making tangible what is often difficult to describe. Additionally, scales offer the possibility of clarifying essential differences when you are determining your position. Discussing progress in concrete terms becomes possible. Soft factors in particular can be brought into the reckoning. And in the team, you can make the differing perceptions and assessments obvious. Differences become visible and can be discussed.

The secret of scaling questions, however, is not in the value of the number on the scale. The number is – as we have already mentioned – always very subjective, and therefore, you cannot compare individual team members' answers. The secret is to use follow-up questions to support and reinforce energy oriented towards the future.

Examples of the Use of Scales

These are the basic steps in working with scales:

Determining your Position

'On a scale of 1 to 10, where 10 is the desired state (incredibly good) and 1 is the absolute opposite, where do you think the team is with respect to this issue today?'

Looking at Past Skills and Resources

'So you are already at point X (no matter whether the situation is assessed at 2, 5, or 7). So what is already working well?'

This enables you to find out small secrets of success in the past. This increases confidence and trust in the possibility of positive developments.

'How did you manage to get to X already? You could be lower than that. But you are already at X. That must have something to do with your abilities and skills?'

This is an invitation to discover small, unnoticed resources and make strengths more transparent and useful for reaching your goal.

Making Goals more Concrete

'What exactly will tell you that you have reached your goal? What exactly will you be doing differently? What will be the consequences?'

With this follow-up question, we aim to find out exactly what individual team members will be doing differently when they have reached their goal. This question creates space for designing a clear and attractive image of the desired future.

Focusing on Next Steps

'What could you do to get a small step further on the scale towards 10?'

Attention is consciously drawn to small steps of improvement. We want to collect a lot of ideas in order to increase the number of choices. As a consequence you gain more clarity on what you could realistically do (a bit) differently. And this in turn offers the opportunity to design tangible measures.

Type 5: Circular Questions

Circular questions help us think out of the box. The questions help us recognise complex patterns of relationships and additionally point out new perspectives. Circular questions clarify multilevel contexts and situations which are the rule in a system (team). The people concerned are not judged or reported on but are recognised as parts of a complicated system of cause and effect.

Circular questions are based on the realisation that there are really no 'if this – then that' explanations. Linear thinking is replaced by circular or linked thinking. A problem is created by the behaviour of several people due to various interdependencies and influences. With circular questions, we explore which actions and behaviours (for example: customer to project manager) are linked to one another and how one person choosing to modify his own behaviour can provide a constructive contribution in the direction of the goal. With circular questions you can test measures for the effects they are going to have.

Circular questions show every individual in the team the far reaching implications his or her modified personal behaviour can have on team performance. They show the effect one's own behaviour has on the behaviour of others.

Useful Questions

- What do you think your colleague Mr H would say to your colleague Ms M about your conflict with your boss?
- What do you think your boss would say to the CEO if you changed your behaviour in this way?
- What would be the implications for your customers if you carried out the project in this way?
- How would the relationship between your colleague and her boss develop if you took up more responsibility for the area that we discussed?
- What would the effects on the performance of your team be if you and Mr S continued to have extensive hostile discussions on this subject?

Type 6: Strange Questions

This kind of question involves a sense of humour, creativity and playfulness. Strange questions are thought-provoking and often create brief irritation with your coaching partner, often in combination with a little chuckle. Used sparingly and at the right moment, they yield surprisingly good results especially in conflict situations. Often the team remembers one of these questions months after the team workshop – because they were strange and thought-provoking.

With these questions it is important that we announce them. You can ask the team for permission to ask such a question. (Has the work so far been helpful? Are we on the right track? – I have a question that might seem a bit strange at first sight. But I have had some very good experiences with it. Do you think I can ask you this question, too?) Announcing a question gives it a special importance.

There is really no recipe for strange questions. You think of one, or you don't. If one occurs to you, that might be a sign that it can be useful. Strange and thought-provoking questions bring a new focus on reality. They can make things talk, personify abstract concepts or integrate very unlikely or miraculous images into work.

Useful Questions

- How would your computer know that you have reached your goal?
- Which object in your daily life could help you to lead meetings in a calmer and in a more goal oriented way?
- How would you know that you had not brought the conflict into the room with you at the next project meeting?
- If, on one of your next mountain hiking tours, you come to a lake and take all of your guilt feelings and attach them to a big stone – and then throw the stone into the lake to vanish forever – what would be different then?
- Suppose your team rules could speak: what would they say about how they are being implemented in this team?
- One thing would be very interesting: how could you make all of this even worse?

General Remarks

There is a broad palette of solution developing questions. Whether a question is useful or helpful generally becomes clear by the reaction of the customer or team. All of these questions have several things in common:

- They are open questions. They cannot be answered with 'Yes' or 'No' but open up room for the conversation. They demand the person asking them as well as the person answering them to think of and formulate new perspectives.

Solution finding questions trigger thought processes that help to develop customised solutions. There are only right answers, increasing choices and not limiting them.

- They are not leading questions that almost prescribe the answer for the client. If you use leading questions, you subliminally convey your own value system of 'right' and 'wrong'. Leading questions take the thoughts of other people in a certain direction – our direction. They are manipulative questions whose goal it is to convince other people of a certain opinion. 'Mr B, don't you also think that in this situation it would really be the smartest thing to …' 'But surely, you will not resign yourself to accepting that …' The SolutionCircle is there to provide a framework, in which the opinions of all team members are accepted and valued. Only then does it become possible to develop results that are customised to the team and not just to the coach / manager.

- They concentrate primarily on visible behaviour – and not on general concepts. If we are talking about better collaboration, success, clear leadership, more cooperation etc., we are interested in what the individual team members will actually be doing when things are better. What exactly is the difference? How will the team know that co-operation has improved? Often the words and concepts are described so differently by each individual that everybody really understands something else when they are used. Therefore, it is not the labels or concepts that are important, but the specific actions that the individuals connect with them. Only then does the change process come alive and relevant for the daily life of the team – if not, you often get stuck with good intentions and empty words.

Pausing for Reflection

The coach leads the meeting throughout. He or she accompanies the team and looks after everybody's well-being, including his or her own, as well as providing direction during the workshop. He or she leads the group as directly as possible towards their desired goal by asking questions.

Inserting short breaks during the workshop to give an opportunity to reflect on the process helps to assess what has already been accomplished and to plan the next steps. Needs, wishes, or even irritations cannot always be recognised from the outside. So what do we do? Ask your employees how much the conversation has contributed so far to getting nearer to the common goal. Questions about how the process is going open the meeting up for feedback and help to keep on track.

These breaks also offer good opportunities to stay in touch with any team members who are critical and improve their acceptance for the responsibility for the solution.

Useful Questions

- How helpful has what we have done so far been in reaching our goal?
- Let's say we were at 1 with regard to our goal at the beginning of this workshop, and the goal that we are aiming at is at 10. Where do you think are we now on that scale?
- What has been helpful so far in getting to this point?
- Where do you think could we get to realistically today?
- What steps do we have to take to achieve that?

Silence and Attentive Awareness

Maybe it is a bit unusual to mention silence and attentive awareness at this point. However, just like in music – which consists mainly of pauses – moments of silence are very important in working with the SolutionCircle. Consciously chosen waiting, silent listening, attentive awareness and accompanying the client, letting silence happen means accepting and integrating passivity and inner reflection. Being silent and talking by turns often seems natural. But if you know how hectic communication can get in many companies, you start to appreciate breaks. Silence also has something to do with letting things happen, stepping out of the pressure to act and letting things emerge. Managers in particular want to have control over everything – and this is exactly why they often lose control. Experience shows that the best solutions develop when you are watching, waiting, after you have almost given up.

Illuminating Small Successes

The change processes with the SolutionCircle build on previous successes and existing resources. The task of the coach is to pay careful attention to competencies and skills and also to talk about and label them. It is important to focus on successes more often – even if they seem very inconspicuous at first.

Ben Furman, a solution-oriented therapist and coach from Finland has developed a simple but efficient tool for this. He calls it the Triple, short for 'The Triple Praise'. The Triple Praise consists of three elements. The first element is called 'The Exclamation of Wonder'. Usually it is a vocalisation that includes the word 'Wow!' followed by the sentence beginning with: 'I am impressed by the way that ...'

The second part of the triple praise is called the 'Statement of

Difficulty'. After the exclamation of wonder you make a statement about how difficult, or hard it is to succeed with something like that. My favourite Statement of Difficulty goes like this: 'That's not easy!' but you can test variations such as 'I would not have been able to do that!' or 'Not everybody can do that!' etc.

The third part of the triple praise is a question, known as the Interrogation of Credit. It is a simple question that seeks to find how success was achieved. My favourite phrasing of the Interrogation of Credit question is: 'How did you do that?' but other options are available for the creative 'triplist'.

The person in the exercise who has reported the success and has had the experience of being the recipient of the Triple responds to the Interrogation of Credit question by 'Sharing Credit'. This means that they have an attack of modesty and generosity and share credit for their success with whoever comes to mind. In effect they are to say something like: 'I'd never have succeeded with this if so and so had not helped me (or supported me or whatever).'

The exercise, however, does not end here. It has a final part. And the final part is called 'Backcreditation'. Yes, you read correctly. Not accreditation but backcreditation. Backcreditation is a new term that refers to the act of giving credit back to the person whom it belongs. There are many phrases you can use to do backcreditation. My favourite one is: 'That's kind of you to thank (him/her/them), but I am sure that you yourself played some part in it too!'

(Source: the Solutions-L listserv 29 August, 2002)

8 Keeping Things Going

'Learning happens where the awareness is.'

Tim Gallwey

You can only determine whether or not working on a turbulent situation has been successful after the team has left the meeting room and is back at work. In order to reach the greatest possible sustainability of the planned change in the team, it is absolutely essential to continue to work on the issues in day-to-day business. The process needs to be kept going in everyday life. There are various ways of doing that. It is important to observe and comment on small changes and successes. In this way team members are encouraged, new behaviour is reinforced and progress becomes visible.

Thinking early on about the way in which progress is to continue has proven to be extremely helpful. In the following you find a few examples that various teams and departments have found useful.

1: Celebrating Progress

Progress Poster
The tax department of the administration of a large city had been struggling with an unpleasant atmosphere among several employees. In order to maintain the process of improved collaboration, the team decided to put up a large poster in the corridor connecting all their offices. On this poster, under the heading 'progress' every

team member noted the progress and successes of the measures they had agreed upon. After two weeks this poster was discussed in the department meeting, and the next steps were planned building on observed progress.

Mail Survey

The sales personnel of an insurance company were stationed in different regions. In order to continue their development process, they decided to send out a mail survey every Thursday containing three questions:

- Have you noticed an improvement in issue Y over the last couple of days? If so, what?
- What did you do to contribute to the improvement?
- What would you like the others to do more of?

Conversations with Supporters

There were nine people in the core team of an architectural company. In the SolutionCircle workshop, they decided that every participant would find an external supporter for the implementation phase. This could be a colleague, an external coach or a knowledgeable acquaintance. They each decided to have two conversations with their supporters, in which the second conversation was to deal explicitly with concrete progress.

Scaling Dance in the Department Meeting

The leading team of a large institution for adult education had set four basic principles for their collaboration. A lot of emphasis was placed on their meeting culture that was deemed to be not very efficient. They decided to check visible progress regularly in their meetings by using scales.

- Where are we now with regard to the implementation of our basic principles?
- How will we be aware of useful change?
- What will take us the next small step forwards?

Project Meetings

A project team in a bank decided that they would hang up the flipchart with the planned measures at the next project meetings. As a fixed item on the agenda (and not at the end of the meeting), they were going to go through the individual measures and talk them over. They would discuss what had already been carried out, exchange success stories and determine where there was a need for further action.

2: A Survey as Additional Reinforcement

External coaches in particular are sometimes faced with the question whether the tools they use have proved to be effective in the every day life of the team.

A research survey has shown to be useful here: several weeks after the first workshop, team members are questioned about visible changes in the team that they attribute to the SolutionCircle. It is exciting to find out what works in day to day life.

You can engage external suppliers to carry out telephone interviews of approximately twenty minutes with every team member. What is surprising about this is that this interview not only yields important information for the external coach but also exerts a constructive influence on the team process. By answering the questions on the telephone, the individual team members are given an additional opportunity to reflect on concrete effects of the workshop and learn from them, which again strengthens the commitment.

The twofold advantage of the telephone interview – we learn more about our own work which is useful for designing future workshops, and at the same time, we can intensify the change process in the team – can keep the process going well without spending too much time on it.

Framework of the Interview

Generally, the interview is conducted by an unrelated professional taking an anonymous record. Normally, the record is then made available only to the external coach. Appointments for the interview are set for every member of the team beforehand. Every team member should have the opportunity to spend twenty minutes on the telephone without being interrupted. It makes most sense to conduct the interviews two or three weeks after the workshop.

Success Stories

Since we assume that it is easier to learn from success, we focus in these interviews on what positive changes have occurred. We are interested in small and large success stories and how the team managed to achieve them. The external coach is sometimes asked by the customer to write a report at the end of the team coaching. The interviews and the success stories contained in them provide a good basis for this progress report.

Possible Interview Questions

- What positive changes have you noticed since the last workshop in the team (regarding the issue X)?
- What would the other team members say was your contribution?
- All in all, how useful was the team workshop on the way to constructive collaboration in the team? (Scale from 1 to 10; 10 = useful beyond anything you could have hoped for; 1 = was not helpful at all!)

- Which elements of the workshop with the SolutionCircle were most useful in the practical implementation?
- What would you especially like for the next workshop (if there is a workshop planned!)?

Example

Three weeks after a one day workshop with a team of fifteen people, all the team members were questioned about the effects of the workshop. The following is an excerpt from one of the interview records:

Have you noticed any positive changes since the last team workshop?

Team leader (TL):

Definitely, we are more careful and honest with one another. For myself, I keep the promises that I made and think about situations that I would have dealt with almost automatically before. Since I am the leader, I also have the responsibility to a model the behaviours I want to encourage, and since I am conscious of this fact, I act accordingly.

Team member A (TA):

Before every department meeting we take our coffee break together. We send around e-mails about who will bring biscuits or sandwiches etc. – and this happens every fortnight. These informal meetings are a good breeding ground for developments towards our goal. This way, we also have a meeting outside the normal problem environment. Previously we only met when there was a problem. We are just now starting to get to know one another.

Team member B (TB):

The way we deal with each other is almost normal, the tone of voice etc. There are only a few that have problems with one another.

What would other team members say you contributed?

TL: I think that other employees are also aware of this change. I am aware that my new actions are noticed. I think that they would say that I am more open. And with new instructions, I take time to order my thoughts first. I think they would say that I approach them more directly now and hide myself in my office less.

TA: You can see my optimism – my glass is half full. In spite of the sword of Damocles that is hanging over me (a restructuring), I seem motivated. I laugh and sometimes I make a joke – I would not have dared to do that before.

TB: I am working harder now to make things run more smoothly. As agreed, I use the to-do list tool very meticulously and responsibly.

All in all, how useful was the team workshop on the way to constructive collaboration in the team? (Scale from 1 to 10; 10 = useful beyond anything you could have hoped for; 1 = was not helpful at all)

TL: 5; it took quite a while, but now something is developing. The atmosphere is much more relaxed since we were able to resolve a lot of conflicts and we are now seeing a common goal in the department. Actually, I would probably have to set it to 7, even. However, many of the difficulties cannot be solved by this kind of coaching. Many strategic issues that have to be decided at the top management level also have to be changed.

TA: 8–9; at last there is a forum that we can use to be together to discuss things, away from individual worries and problems and towards a common view. We are now able to see the meta-level. Additionally, we see our own roles in the whole organisation more clearly and this is very motivating and helps us to see that our problems are relative. What was exciting for me was how easily things can be implemented in our work – even right away.

TB: 8 – Actually, I would like to say 10. It was very useful on the interpersonal level, even if technical things are not yet running as smoothly as they should. The interpersonal level is more important, though, and I think we profited a lot from the coaching here.

Which elements of the SolutionCircle workshop were most useful in the practical implementation?

TL: The Future Perfect, clearly. A first glimpse of the ideal state – and suddenly your ideal becomes more tangible and you discover the steps that are still missing to get to the goal, and hey – it becomes feasible!!!

TA: Looking into the future: a day in 5 years time. For me this was a totally new approach. I realised that it was difficult for almost everybody to let go of today, let problems rest and look positively to the future. For me this was a necessary step outside the system.

TB: Switching to the level of solution helped us to relax and to turn our perspective to what is possible. (At the end he said, wow, there is so much potential for improvement!)

Has your way of discussing things in the team changed? What has made you notice this difference?

TL: People are willing to let things go. Even if everything is not straightened out, they can communicate normally and are able to co-operate – things are simply more relaxed.

TA: This morning in the meeting everybody behaved well even though the stakes were high. People hear each other out much more than before.

TB: The atmosphere is very different. This Monday's meeting cannot be compared to the ones we had before. The discussion was on a much higher level, but we also realised that there is some danger of falling back into old habits. I guess that having the meetings in the same room as before might not be a great way to attempt a new start. It is much easier for people to take up a new role if the external environment changes, too.

What characteristics of the external coach did you find most helpful?

TL: He listened very well. He didn't just hit us over the head with a solution. His thoughts and ideas were very thoughtful and relevant to us. He had the ability to separate what is important from what is unimportant.

TA: Asking: 'What is your contribution?' and especially that he was very persistent. He was determined and still stayed elegantly at the level of goals. There was no way of moving him from it.

TB: He was very neutral (TB appreciated the agreement that the group was to let the coach know if they found him biased – but it did not turn out to be necessary). He was not judgmental, listened, was calm and showed an interest in people. He had a clear concept of how it was going to work out.

3: The Follow-up Workshop

Shorter follow-up workshops are a common means of keeping progress going and amplifying it. In two or three hours, the group exchanges the progress they achieved together, clarifies what needs to be clarified and determines the next steps.

In the follow-up workshop, you usually need only the following elements of the SolutionCircle:

Highlights: Since the last workshop, what has improved?

Scaling Dance: Where is the team today? How did the team manage to get to this point?

Steps: What are the next steps? How do we keep the process going?

Personal Mission: What should each team member focus his or her attention on?

Possible Agenda for a Follow-up Meeting

Goals
- We want to find out what has improved since the last workshop.
- We want to be clear about the talents and skills that have got us this far.

After the workshop, the team knows where we stand with regard to individual measures and where we might need corrections and adjustments.

Introduction
Clarifying the goals of this workshop.
Remembering our agreements (clarifying the framework – rules of collaboration).
Any other necessary preliminaries.

Highlights

What is better since the last workshop (gather lists individually or together in groups)?

Illuminating resources: how did we do that? What and who helped us with it?

What worked?

What else improved?

And what else?

Scaling Dance

Illuminating Progress

If we take our well-known scale (10 stands for the future perfect and 1 for the opposite) – where does everybody stand now?

The participants assess the situation on the scale, so that the assessments can be verified by questions and everybody understands what they mean:

- What were the most important milestones for you on the way to X?
- What are you doing better now?
- What would you like to keep doing in the future?
- What could we learn for the future from our different perceptions?

Scaling Confidence

How confident is everyone that the team will be able to keep this process going successfully?

Where on the scale will you be satisfied regarding topic X?

How confident are you that you will be able to reach this point?

Where does this confidence come from?

What tells you that you can be this sure?

What do you need to make you a bit more confident?

Designing The Next Steps

At this point, it is important to determine together which steps are best taken next, which steps are going to be continued, which new steps designed and how exactly one will go about it. It is helpful to test exactly how useful these measures are going to be. What exactly should they achieve? And how do I, or the team, or the people outside the team recognise that these measure have been successful?

Wrap-up

At the end of the process, we need to find out what the individual team members need in order to keep things constructive and carry out the measures agreed upon. Sometimes nothing more is needed – in other cases, teams offer specific suggestions that could be helpful in addition to what has already been discussed.

4: SolutionSurfing in the Team's Daily Life

'Be the change you want to see in the world.'

Mahatma Gandhi

SolutionSurfing wants to make working in a team easy and target-oriented. The individual elements of the SolutionCircle can be integrated into the leadership repertoire as efficient tools. This way, you can integrate the power of solution- and resource-oriented working principles into the daily life of your team.

Here are a few practical examples:

Scaling Dance in Employee Appraisals

Frank has been manager of the control department of a large bank for a couple of years. He hopes to be able to raise the social competence of the individual employees by introducing different scales into conversations about soft skills. Quantitative values like turnover, sales figures or on-time completion of projects can be assessed objectively relatively easily. Soft skills like the ability to co-operate, flexibility, power of innovation and so on, can be made transparent using scales.

- On a scale of 1 to 10, how do you assess your leadership performance in the project?
- What did you do specifically to get to that point?
- Where were you last year regarding your leadership competence?
- Where would like to get to on the scale with regard to your leadership competence?
- When you have reached this number, what exactly will you be doing differently then? How will your employees know?
- What could be a first small step in the direction of your goal number?

Simple numbers are used to facilitate orientation, to make the soft skills more concrete. Scaling makes clear positioning possible and enables us to illuminate progress and to formulate goals.

Future Perfect in Setting up an Association

Peter and two of his friends wanted to set up an association to organise national events for large audiences. When the three were sitting together for the first time, they agreed on a small role play: they imagined that the meeting was taking place two years after the founding of the association. They 'beamed' into the future in their thoughts and exchanged their views on what they had achieved and where they were seeing problems in a fictitious board meeting.

The three found this a very agreeable way of working. In addition, each of them developed a very specific image of what he wanted from this association, which goals were central, what gave confidence that they would be able to reach these goals – and it also showed them where the stumbling blocks could be. Additionally it became clear where the energies of each member lay and what they were enthusiastic about.

This way, the next steps could be planned and tackled in detail by the three friends.

Discussing past activities of a project from a future perspective sharpens our image of the goal and opens things up to new ideas. This phenomenon is known from sports: top athletes report how many competitions are won almost exclusively in the mind. Marathon runners carry themselves through the toughest times by imagining how they will run over the finish line. They put themselves into the situation in which they will have done it, heard the shouts and cheers of the crowd, and raised their hands with enthusiasm on the finish line. The joy and satisfaction of this drives them on. This is surely much more helpful than concentrating on their pain and tiredness. Letting yourself be led by the desired future can be a useful starting point in projects and activities.

Expectations and Goals in a Department Meeting

A team of experts in the IT department agreed to hold half of the department meeting as an open meeting. Every participant would have the opportunity to bring up topics that were important to him or her. The guiding question was: 'What needs to be discussed/ decided in this meeting to make it worth my time?' The procedure agreed upon consisted of two steps:

a) If you want to discuss a topic with the other participants, you introduce it briefly in two sentences and say what you want to achieve at the end of the discussion (goal). In addition, you mention how much time you expect the topic to take.

b) The individual topics, including goals and time needed, are put down on a flipchart and are prioritised together. Every team member can assign three, two, or one points.

Solution-Oriented Questions in a Project Meeting

Gordon was an external consultant leading a large IT project in local government administration. The project team was made up of county employees, external software suppliers and representatives of the future users of the new software. Gordon had become used to asking solution developing questions since he discovered that they can save a lot of time and energy.

Supplier:	I'm sorry to say that we haven't been able to test the first version of the software yet because our tester was sick and the other employees are already complaining about being totally overworked. In addition, the deadline came at rather short notice.
Gordon:	Can you tell me when it will be possible to finish the first testing phase that was planned for today?
Supplier:	Well, difficult to say. Our boss said that it was not so urgent and as I just said, on top of everything, one of our colleagues got ill.
Gordon:	OK. Do you need anything from any of us to carry out the tests?
Supplier:	Not really, we have to deal with this internally.
Gordon:	Agreed. So when will it be possible for you to finish testing? Give me a realistic assessment.
Supplier:	We should be done in ten days.
Gordon:	I am relying on you. So you will have it on the 14th. What does this mean for the rest of the project?

Gordon concentrated entirely on what was wanted. The question of 'why' did not enter the discussion. Also, he did not respond to the gentle reproach about the 'short notice deadline'. He consistently focused on the solution and then checked the effects of the new suggestion. In every project, there are numerous reasons why something does not happen the way it had been planned. If you stay at the level of solutions, you can save huge amounts of time. In addition, Gordon rejected the responsibility for this part of the project and simply expected that everybody was doing their job and developing solutions for his or her problems.

5: The SolutionCircle in Change and Development Processes

A team of marketing specialists had been using elements of the SolutionCircle for their team development. Two new members had joined the group a little more than two months previously and they had to be integrated. In addition to that, there was a need for a reorganisation of the whole marketing agency.

The team used the following elements for their first workshop:

Expectations and Goals
What do we want to achieve today? How will we know that we have reached our goal today?

Highlights
What are we already doing successfully and what would we like to continue doing in the future?

Future Perfect
What will our team look like in six months time? What exactly will we be doing then? How will we describe our success then?

Steps
What do the first concrete steps helping us to move towards the future perfect look like?

In order to keep the process going, the team agreed that

- everybody would have a conversation with somebody outside the marketing business in order to have a critical view on the ideas discussed;
- they would report on that in a department meeting in two weeks time;
- a large poster would be put up in the cafeteria, listing intermediary steps in the implementation of the measures.

Four weeks after the first workshop the team met for a second session that started with the question: 'What has happened in the last few weeks that is already taking us in the direction of our image of the future?'

Start of the Department Meeting

A team of consultants who work with job-seeking managers start their weekly team meeting with two standard questions:

- What was the highlight of my work last week?
- How can we use these discoveries in order to continue to optimise the quality of our consultancy?

Scenes from School Teachers' Away Day

The morning of the first day of the annual retreat was billed as 'Looking back and looking forward'. The team leader had drawn a scale of 1 to 10 on a big piece of paper. Every teacher now set a dot on the number on the scale that described best where they stood at the moment. A second dot was placed on the number that they would like to achieve. A third dot was put on a number that signified an occasion in the last year when they felt better than now (a highlight of the last year).

They exchanged their views on the following questions in groups of two:

- What contributes to the fact that I am at number X now? What else?
- What exactly was different in my highlight? What did I contribute to it?
- What could I do to move a little closer to the state that I would like?

In the end, the team leader formulated a very elegant personal task. She asked every team member to predict where they would be on the scale in four weeks. How would they know that they are on the predicted number? What would their colleagues notice?

Every member wrote down the answers to these questions. In four weeks, in their regular teachers' conference, they would check their prognoses and exchange views on them.

6: Basic Structure of Team Coaching

The tax administration department of a large City had problems with 'bad atmosphere'. The team of six woman produced excellent results; however, most of them thought the atmosphere at work was bad. The team hired an external coach, who structured the procedure like this:

First Workshop 4 hours followed by dinner	• Clarifying framework, rules of collaboration • Formulating goals and making them concrete • Identifying Hot Topics, building interest groups • Scaling Dance: positioning • Future Perfect in interest groups • Designing first small steps • Observation task
Telephone Interview 3 weeks after the first workshop	Telephone Interview with every team member (about 20 minutes): • What positive changes have you noticed? • What early successes? • What did you contribute? • What could help to continue on that path? • Scaling: before the first workshop and today? What is the difference?
Second Workshop approximately 2 weeks after the telephone interview. Duration: 4 hours	• Highlights of the last 2 weeks? • Scaling Dance: positioning today, what worked? • Designing additional measures • Short break: What else does the team need? • …

9 External Consultants

'You cannot teach a man anything; you can only help him discover it in himself.'

Galileo Galilei

Using External Consultants: The Manager's Perspective

In certain situations it can make sense to call in a coach or consultant to deal with problems in the team. In conflict situations where the manager him- or herself is personally concerned, it is a relief for everybody if you ask an external person to facilitate. An outsider can support the team in clarifying conflicts or starting to tackle drastic change processes, especially at the beginning. An external coach can convey a sense of security. Over time it becomes easier for the team to deal with their own difficulties – to leave the problem focus behind.

There are also high performance teams that call in a coach they trust once or twice a year in order to see things from a different perspective and to make further steps of development more concrete.

Generally you can say that an external coach can be deployed

- to start a (change) process;
- if the manager and team are not able to steer the process and take part in it at the same time;
- if difficult or embarrassing conflicts need to be solved, in which the management plays an important role;

- if there is a high emotional involvement of the people concerned;
- if the team is stuck;
- if the same problems emerge regularly;
- to take the strain off the team manager;
- to get an outside perspective on progress.

What can an external coach achieve?

No coach can make a team successful! That is something it has to accomplish itself. The content of the team's work is not the subject matter of the coaching. The process of collaboration between the team members is. The coach provides the framework to enable everybody to enter into a target-oriented conversation with one another.

Important output of a coach

- asking many target-oriented questions;
- observing what happens between the team members when they are working;
- making new ways of seeing possibilities;
- defining specific goals with the team;
- selecting measures and interventions that enable the team to reach its goals in the best possible way;
- testing whether the team is on track toward a customised solution;
- stimulating new patterns of thinking.

A coach will never

- take over leadership, but will instead be helpful to management and every team member;

- reproach the group for mistakes, but will instead help it to discover strengths;
- take decisions for the team, but will instead pave the way for them;
- meddle with the content of the work;
- make the team dependent on him- or herself, but will instead encourage them to become independent of outside help.

A good coach has a lot of sensitivity. He or she can offer broad experience, professional knowledge and solution focus; and it is these abilities and experiences that the team bought when hiring him or her. In many phases, an outsider can be extremely useful for coping with turbulent situations. In the end, however, every team has to find the necessary ability and vitality to perform from the inside.

From Contact to Contract: The External Consultant's Perspective

'Leading by Asking'

The telephone rings, and a potential customer asks whether we can help. She is looking for an external coach to design a workshop together with her team. This is how it often begins. A first contact is made and the next step would be an agreement to collaborate.

When an external coach is invited in by a team, he or she encounters a whole new world. He or she does not know the actors, nor their history, nor their way of working and communicating. He or she knows hardly anything about the environment or about the previous efforts made by the team to find a solution. And even after the best initial contact and follow-up conversation, a lot will remain unclear. This is why we put less weight on analysing the problem and start focusing on the goals of the collaboration as quickly and as specifically as possible. What is important is that the hiring manager and the coach understand one another concerning the task at hand.

Some companies are more concrete than others when it comes to communicating what improvements they expect after working with an external coach: often they know exactly where they want improvement – and often they do not.

This is why solution-developing questions are very effective in the first conversation clarifying the situation. They are aimed at gaining information and clarifying the goals. At the same time, you create new knowledge: not only does the person asking solution-developing questions gain more information, but so does the person answering them.

Types of Question in the Initial Conversation

Solution-Developing Questions

- What would you like to develop? What is your goal?
- How would you know that the consultation has been successful?
- What would you/others gain from a successful consultation?
- If this coaching were to be very successful, what exactly would be different?
- What else?
- ...

Questions about the Company

- How is the company doing in general?
- What does organisational structure look like? What are the reporting lines?
- What is this team responsible for?
- What is the reason for this coaching?
- ...

Resource Questions

- What has the team achieved successfully recently?
- What would another team/other colleagues/customers say is a special strength of this team?
- What do you especially appreciate about your team?

Circular Questions

- What do you think your boss thinks about your department?
- ...

Questions about Neutrality

- What role do you think the coach/consultant should play?
- How might the coach lose his or her neutrality?
- ...

Highlights

- When were things better?
- What was different when things were better?
- ...

Stumbling Blocks in the Initial Conversation

It can happen suddenly and it is not very encouraging: an initial conversation goes wrong. Here a few ways of making this more likely:

- Put on your expert glasses and see immediately what is good for the customer.

- Praise your own ideas at the first possible opportunity.
- Ask the customer questions without asking for permission.
- Let the conversation flow along aimlessly.
- Put both of you under time pressure.
- Guarantee success and take responsibility for it.
- Go too fast.
- Ignore what your own body tells you.
- End the conversation without knowing what happens next.
- Let the customer determine the design of the workshop.
- Take lots of stuff with you to the initial conversation, like folders with presentation material, notebook, beamer, cables and a very impressive briefcase...
- Avoid talk of your fee.

(Source: W. Geisbauer, ReTeaming-Handbook)

Have you any other ideas?

The Ideal First Conversation

There is no such thing as an ideal first conversation because every customer is different and every meeting is different. What is important is that the coach knows where he or she is going regarding the commission during the conversation. Structuring the conversation into the following phases can be helpful.

Introduction to the Topic and Clarifying the Situation

In this phase, the customer has the floor. The coach asks questions, writes down the essential information and tries to tune into the customer.

Interview

The coach initiates this phase by asking the customer whether he can ask a couple of questions. The following points can be clarified here:

- Possible clarification of the context (areas of responsibility of the team, organisational structure etc.)
- Solution-developing questions (clarifying goal, resources etc.)

What Would the Customer like to Know About the Coach?

In this phase, the coach gives the customer the opportunity to ask about his or her background, education, experience, references etc.

- What else would you like to know?
- Is there anything I forgot?

Clarifying Organisational Questions

- Where and when will the first meeting be?
- Who should be invited to the workshop?
- How is the team going to be informed?
- How often do we meet and for how long?
- Fees

Clarifying Next Steps

- Who will be responsible for what?
- What are the next steps?

Checklist for Clarifying Conversations

Has the goal been formulated clearly by the customer and do both parties accept it?	
What does the customer expect to gain from a successful consultation?	
Are there unequivocal criteria for the success of the coaching?	
What resources of the team do we know about?	
What successful achievements can the team look back on?	
What attempts at a solution has the customer already made?	
How successful were these attempts?	
Has the working framework been fixed (Time, duration, dates . . .)?	
How will the participants (team) be informed about the consultation?	
Are the fees clear?	
Does the coach feel autonomous regarding the customer and the respective team?	
Is there a written confirmation of the commission including the acceptance of the general terms of business (cancellation procedure and expenses)?	
Is everything clear enough that the coach can start working productively?	
Does the coach know what he or she would like to learn from this job?	

Postscript .... Thanks ... and a Little Game

The end of this tool book is also a new beginning: the beginning of your unique and very personal use of the individual elements of the SolutionCircle, the beginning of your SolutionSurfing.

The challenge for you as a leader is to step out of your usual leadership role and try something new. Competency in using solution-developing tools needs curiosity about situations in your daily life when you can use them – and it needs practice.

Start today, maybe with some simple solution-developing questions and observe how they work. This way you continuously gain more confidence and serenity. I am convinced that you are going to have many experiences of success, big and small, and that you will be able to contribute crucially to the performance of your team.

Thank you ...

I do not know whether it is possible to write a book alone. In my case, I am grateful for the support of several people. I was able to tap the experience and knowledge of several solution-focused people: Insoo Kim Berg, Steve de Shazer, Sonja Radatz, Jürgen Hargens, Ben Furman, Tim Gallwey. Their books, articles and seminars gave me the confidence to continue on this track and finish writing the book. First and foremost I would like to thank Peter Szabó who opened the door to working this way and who supported me with his incredible trust after I had searched for a long time. And I would also like to thank Kati Hankovsky, Philipp Oechsli and Romi Staub for their support.

Jörg Meier accompanied me as a writing coach. I was very happy about his critical, sensitive and detailed feedback.

Kirsten Dierolf and Jenny Clarke made the English version possible – thanks to them both for sensitive translation and sensible restructuring.

And last but not least, Barbara, Till and Res, who gave me space for the phases of intensive writing. Thank you all!

... a Little Game:

I would like to leave you with a little game at the end. You need two small objects like coins or wooden beads – and a bit of curiosity. I often use this game in seminars, not only because it is fun but also because perhaps it shows a basic skill that is very useful in SolutionSurfing. Have fun!

Anna chases Mo (A path to more serenity)

Object of the Game:
Anna wins if she can catch Mo before her 7th turn by occupying the place that Mo is occupying.

Rules:
1: Anna starts.
2: Anna and Mo take turns moving.
3: Anna and Mo can only move along a straight line to a neighbouring spot.
4: Neither Anna nor Mo can jump.

Note : Mo does not stand a chance in this game – provided that Anna plays intelligently.

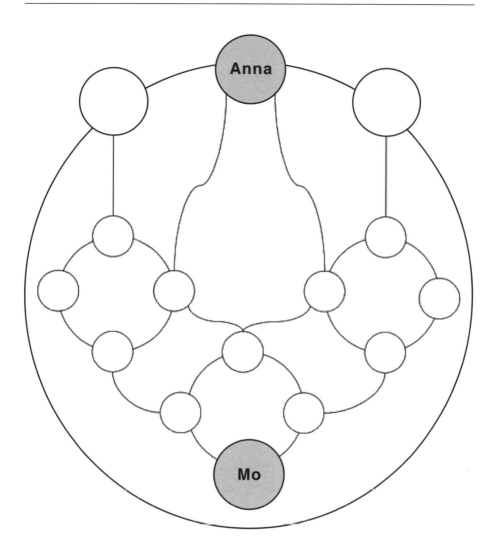

Appendix

Overview of the Steps in the SolutionCircle

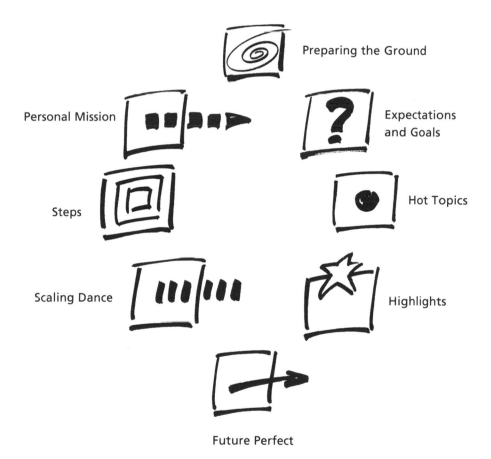

Preparing the Ground

Personal Mission

Expectations and Goals

Steps

Hot Topics

Scaling Dance

Highlights

Future Perfect

Preparing the Ground

Goal

This first step serves to clarify the framework, to gain trust in the coach and agree on what is necessary for everybody to commit to collaborate enthusiastically.

Procedure

Clarify what brought us here.
Name resources that are already apparent to an outsider.
Keep an eye on the solution.
Clarify roles.
Establish groundrules.

Helpful questions

- What rules of communication should we follow in this workshop so that everybody can participate comfortably?
- How will you know that we are discussing things factually and not emotionally? What are we doing when we discuss this way? What are we not doing?
- Does everybody agree that we base our work today on these rules?

Expectations and Goals

Goal

The goal of this step is to define the criteria for the success of the meeting. What goals have to be reached and what expectations have to be fulfilled to make participation worthwhile?

Procedure

Collect expectations and goals on a flipchart.

Helpful questions

- What needs to happen in this workshop to make it really worth your time here?
- What should be different after the workshop?
- How will you know that you have reached this goal?
- If you reach this goal together, how will your customers notice?
- How probable is it in your view that your expectations of the workshop can be met?

Hot Topics

Goal

In this step, we determine the topics where improvement is aimed for.

Procedure

List areas for improvement.

Clarify.

Cluster ideas into groups.

List Hot Topics.

Participants sign up to topics which interest them.

Highlights

Goal

The participants start looking for situations in which the problem or the conflict either did not happen at all or was less severe. They find out which skills enabled them to accomplish this.

Procedure

Collect highlights.

Clarify.

Acknowledge and reinforce resources.

Helpful questions:

- Which events in the last few weeks seem like a small highlight with regard to the issue at hand?
- What exactly was different?
- What did you contribute to enabling your colleague to react this way?
- If you say that you cannot find a highlight in the last months, maybe there was a situation in which the conflict was less severe? What did you contribute to that – what did others contribute?
- What can we learn from these highlights for the solution of the problem?

Future Perfect

Goal

In the future perfect, the team designs a very precise picture of a future in which the problems have been solved.

Procedure

The future perfect is tackled by the interest groups that formed in the Hot Topics step. These groups are given the task of describing the ideal future of their topic as precisely as possible and writing it down.

Helpful questions:

- If we were very successful in this workshop and if the team could develop exactly as we want it to – where would the team be in two years time?
- What exactly would be different?
- What would the customers say about this team?
- If I meet the team again for some reason in two years time, what would I see, that told me something had changed for the better?

Scaling Dance

Goal

The individual team members assess the current situation. We want to find out what has already worked well in the past.

Procedure

The coach can draw the scales on a flipchart or mark them with tape on the floor. The participants then set markers or position themselves on a suitable place on the walking scale.

Helpful questions

- Imagine a scale from 1 to 10. Where are you now with regard to the topic X where 10 stands for the ideal state (future perfect) and 1 stands for the exact opposite?
- How did you manage to get to this point? What is the difference between 1 and where you are now?
- If you think about your best highlight, where was it on the same scale. What is the difference here?
- What did you personally contribute to get you to X?
- How would you know that you have progressed just a small step towards 10?
- Which resources did you use to be able keep at X and not sink lower?

Steps

Goal

In this step we design concrete measures that the team can implement in the near future – the sooner the better.

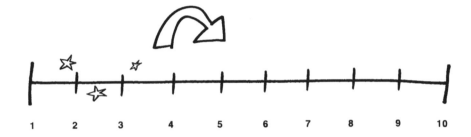

Helpful questions

- What do you need to get one step closer to 10?
- What can you contribute to move things forward a bit?
- How would you notice that the situation has changed just a little bit for the better?
- If this scale could talk, what would it recommend as your next step?
- What would your customers say if you implement this measure? How would your customers notice the difference?
- How are you going to exchange and note the first small successes in the implementation?

Personal Mission

Goal

By giving an observation task or an action-oriented task, attention is directed to certain aspects of the implementation which continue supporting the process in the team's day-to-day life.

Procedure

Observation task.

Every team member commits to take a concrete measure in the very near future.

Bibliography

Books and papers

De Jong, Peter and Berg, Insoo Kim (1998) *Interviewing for Solutions* Brooks/Cole Publishing Company, Pacific Grove, ISBN 0–534–23160–8

von Foerster, Heinz and Pörksen, Bernhard (1998) *Die Wahrheit ist die Erfindung eines Lügners. Gespräche für Skeptiker* Carl Auer, Heidelberg

Furman, Ben and Ahola, Tapani (2001) *Solution Talk: Hosting Therapeutic Conversations* BT Press, ISBN 1871697786

Furman, Ben (1998) *It's Never too Late to Have a Happy Childhood* BT Press, ISBN 1871697727

Gallwey, Tim (2002) *The Inner Game of Work* Random House Trade Paperbacks, ISBN 0375758178

Geisbauer, W, *ReTeaming Handbook* Private communication

Glaserfeld, E. v. u. a. (2002) *Einführung in den Konstruktivismus* Verlag Pieper GmbH Munich, ISBN 3-492–21165–8

Hargens, Jürgen (2002) *Erfolgreich führen und leiten, das will ich auch können …* Borgmann Publishing GmbH, Dortmund, ISBN 3–86145–228–6

Jackson, Paul Z. and McKergow, Mark (2002) *The Solutions Focus: The SIMPLE Way to Positive Change* Nicholas Brealey Publishing, London ISBN 1–85788–270–9

Loistl, Otto (1996) *Chaos – zur Theorie nichtlinearer dynamischer Systeme* Oldenburg R. Verlag GmbH, ISBN 3–486–23813–2

Mussmann, Dr. Carin and Zbinden, Dr. Reto (2003) *Lösungsorientiert Führen und Beraten* KV Zurich, ISBN 2–906607–3

Pörksen, Bernhard (2001) *Abschied vom Absoluten* Carl Auer System Verlag Heidelberg, ISBN 5–140–61080–9

Radatz, Sonja (2000) *Beratung ohne Ratschlag* Institut für Systemisches Coaching und Training, Vienna, ISBN 3–902155–00–0

Rauen, Christopher (2003) *Coaching* Hogrefe/BRO, ISBN 3–8017–1478–0

Schreyögg, Astrid (1996) *Coaching* Campus, Frankfurt, ISBN 3–593–37332–7

de Shazer, Steve (1988) *Clues: Investigating Solutions in Brief Therapy* W. W. Norton, New York, ISBN 0–393–70054–2

Staub, Romi (2002) *Coaching ... und Veränderungen gehen viel einfacher* Fachpublikation HRM-Dossier, Verlag SPEKTRAmedia, Zürich

Szabó, Dr. Peter (2003) *Strategie-Umsetzung und Coaching* in INDEX Betriebswirtschaft 2/2003 S. 24 ff.

Szabó, Dr. Peter (2005) "About solutions-focused scaling: 10 minutes for performance and learning" in Positive Approaches to Change: Applications of Solutions Focus and Appreciative Inquiry at Work edited by Mark McKergow and Jenny Clarke SolutionsBooks, ISBN 0–954–97490 –5

Watzlawick, Paul (1977) *How Real is Real?* Vintage, ISBN 0–394–72256–6

Watzlawick, Paul (1983) *The Situation is Hopeless, But Not Serious: The Pursuit of Unhappiness* W. W. Norton

Whitmore, John (2002) *Coaching for Performance: A Practical Guide to Growing Your Own Skills* Nicholas Brealey Publishing ISBN 1–85788–013–7

zur Bonsen, Matthias and Maleh, Carol (2001) *Appreciative Inquiry* Beltz Verlag – Weinheim und Basel

Links

Systemic/solution focused work with organisations
www.solutionsurfers.com
Solution focused management and consultancy

www.thesolutionsfocus.com
Solution-focused applications in a business context with many additional links all over the world (Mark McKergow and Paul Z. Jackson)

www.isct.at
Institute for Systemic Coaching and Training (Sonja Radatz)

www.solution-focused-management.com
Valuable background information and examples of applications (Louis Cauffman)

Coaching
www.theinnergame.com
Website of Tim Gallwey, with information about his books

www.coachfederation.org
Website of the ICF (International Coach Federation) with links to coaches in the whole world. Hints about the ICF Certifications and international conferences

Training of Solution focused coaching in Switzerland
www.weiterbildungsforum.ch

Solution-focused Brief Therapy
www.brief-therapy.org
Background information, books and videos about solution-focused brief therapy from the Brief Family Therapy Center (Steve de Shazer and Insoo Kim Berg)

About the Author

Daniel Meier

Daniel Meier (1963) is married and has two sons. After training as a teacher, he continued his education in Game Pedagogy and Adult Education (Dipl.-Erwachsenenbildner, AEB Lucerne) and in General Management (WWZ UNI Basel). He worked in and led various teams for several years. Since 2001, he has been coaching managers, teams and organisations in complex development processes, always on the lookout for customised solutions. He leads a coaching company, which accompanies teams and individuals in development processes. Additionally, he offers education and training in solution-oriented coaching.

Daniel Meier is also co-founder of the SolutionSurfers, an association of professional coaches dealing with the question of how you can work and learn more easily and more efficiently in companies. SolutionSurfers see the world as a challenging and exciting landscape for learning and development and they see themsleves as guides for target-oriented, joyful and exciting learning and working. They work as consultants to companies, offer open seminars and develop efficient and practical tools.

More information is available at:
www.solutionsurfers.com or directly by contacting Daniel at
d.meier@solutionsurfers.com

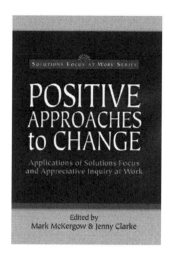

ABOUT SOL

Solutions in Organisations Linkup

Sharing and building Solutions Focused practice in organisations

SOL organises conferences and events around the world to help people join the growing movement to use Solutions Focused ideas at work, in consulting, managing, training, HR practice, strategic planning, performance management, team building and organisational development. The first conference was in February 2002 in Bristol, UK, hosted by Bristol Solutions Group.

For us, sharing is the key word. The originators of the approach, Steve de Shazer and Insoo Kim Berg, have not trade marked their work. Indeed, the SF approach itself is based on collaboration.

It is important to us that SOL retains this generosity of spirit and the collaborative ethos. No-one owns the Solutions in Organisations Link-up name. We do not favour a membership based organisation with the corresponding administrative costs and duties. SOL is not a membership organization. You can join in by participating in SOL events, and/or joining the SOL email discussion group listserver, SOLUTIONS-L.

SOL is run voluntarily by an international steering group. The group meets at SOL International Conferences - if you are interested in getting involved, come to a conference, or contact one of the group in advance.

Anyone is free to organize an event under the SOL banner, as long as it is in line with the SOL Charter and has the support of the international steering group. If you have an idea for an event, whether it be geographically based (ie a national or regional event) or subject-matter oriented (focusing on a particular application of solution focused work), get in touch with any member of the steering group via

www.solworld.org

Index